KITH AND KIN AND THE LIVED EXPERIENCE OF PERSONS WITH INTELLECTUAL DISABILITIES

This book considers the ways in which the lives of persons with intellectual disability are closely interconnected with those of the persons around them. The ways in which these interconnections work and the effects they have are examined by taking a very close look at specific instances in the lives of persons with intellectual disability, taken from published research and other sources and covering various life domains, including education, employment, creative work, socialising and family life.

The fourteen case-study chapters (covering Australia, France, Ireland, Italy, Malta, Spain, the UK and the USA) focus on the interactions between the person with intellectual disability concerned and other persons. The analyses use Paul Ricoeur's concept of the interrelational self to show how the lives and selves of persons with intellectual disability are intimately intertwined with those of the persons who come into contact with them. Furthermore, it is argued that what we learn about the deep connections between persons with intellectual disability and those who play a significant role in their lives can be applied to general human experience. What happens in each one-to-one interaction is of paramount importance. The analyses are also based on Max Van Manen's phenomenological research approach and critical phenomenology. The innovative approach thus created provides fresh insights and a different method for carrying out research and analysis in the area.

The short format of the chapters in the main part of the book makes it suitable for use on a wide range of courses in disability studies as well as in other disciplines and areas of study, such as psychology, education, legal studies and childhood studies among others. It also makes it accessible for advocates and practitioners working with persons with intellectual disability.

Anne-Marie Callus is Associate Professor in the Department of Disability Studies, Faculty for Social Wellbeing, University of Malta. She lectures, researches and has published on disability rights, empowerment of persons with intellectual disability, inclusive education, and disabled children's rights, as well as cultural representations of persons with disability. She is Deputy Editor of *Disability & Society*.

KITH AND KIN AND THE LIVED EXPERIENCE OF PERSONS WITH INTELLECTUAL DISABILITIES

Anne-Marie Callus

Routledge
Taylor & Francis Group
LONDON AND NEW YORK

Designed cover image: Getty image number 1371108369

First published 2026
by Routledge
4 Park Square, Milton Park, Abingdon, Oxon OX14 4RN

and by Routledge
605 Third Avenue, New York, NY 10158

Routledge is an imprint of the Taylor & Francis Group, an informa business

British Library Cataloguing-in-Publication Data
A catalogue record for this book is available from the British Library

ISBN: 978-1-032-77606-4 (hbk)
ISBN: 978-1-032-91155-7 (pbk)
ISBN: 978-1-003-56164-4 (ebk)

DOI: 10.4324/9781003561644

Typeset in Sabon
by Apex CoVantage, LLC

I dedicate this book to the memory of
Marthese Deguara

CONTENTS

LIST OF PERMISSIONS

Chapter 1 excerpt taken from *Klara and the Sun* by Kazuo Ishiguro. Published by Faber & Faber, 2021. Copyright © Kazuo Ishiguro. Reproduced by permission of the author c/o Rogers, Coleridge & White Ltd., 20 Powis Mews, London W11 1JN.

Chapter 2 excerpt taken from p. 31 of Diana Tsokova and Jane Tarr, 2012. *Diverse Perspectives on Inclusive School Communities*. Taylor & Francis. Used with permission of Taylor & Francis.

Chapter 3 excerpt taken from Inclusion Europe, 2020. *Customised employment*. YouTube https://www.youtube.com/watch?v=4hVg4K65KCA. Used with permission of Inclusion Europe.

Chapter 4 excerpt reproduced from Godefroy Lansade. De la difficulté à être reconnus « capables » et « compétents » : des adolescents et jeunes adultes désignés handicapés mentaux en quête d'autonomie. The difficulty of being recognized as 'capable' and 'competent': Adolescents and young adults designated as mentally disabled in search of autonomy. *Alter: European Journal of Disability Research*, 13(1), pp. 29–42. Copyright © 2019, Alter, European Society for Disability Research, published by Elsevier Masson SAS. All rights reserved. Translated version from the original French used with permission of the author.

Chapter 5 photograph from pp. 98–99 of Graham Miller, 2013. *Six Percent – Down's Syndrome: My Photographs their Stories*. Photohonesty. Reproduced with permission of Graham Miller, and Eve and Lesley.

Chapter 6 excerpt taken from pp. 131–132 of G. Mazzariol, 2020. *Mio Fratello Rincorre I Dinosauri* [*My Brother Chases Dinosaurs*]. © 2016 and 2018 Giulio Einaudi editore s.p.a., Turin. Own translation from the original Italian.

Chapter 7 excerpt taken from episode 176 of *DNA Today: A Genetics Podcast*, hosted and produced by Kira Dineen, MS, LCGC, CG(ASCP) CM. http://dnapodcast.com/episodes/2022/3/18/176-glees-lauren-potter-on-down-syndrome-awareness. Used with permission of DNA Today.

Chapter 8 excerpt taken from p. 151 of M. C. Dunn, I. C. Clare and A. J. Holland, 2010. Living 'a life like ours': Support workers' accounts of substitute decision-making in residential care homes for adults with intellectual disabilities. *Journal of Intellectual Disability Research*, 54(2), pp. 144–160. Used with permission from John Wiley & Sons.

Chapter 9 poem by Noelle Doran, Me. In *Pen & Palette: A Selection of Poetry and Paintings by Students of the National Institute for Intellectual Disability, Trinity College Dublin*, p. 18. Used with permission of the National Institute for Intellectual Disability and Noelle Doran.

Chapter 10 excerpt taken from pp. 44–45 of Marika Abela, 2012. *The Social Inclusion of Students with Moderate to Severe Disabilities in a Boys' Comprehensive Secondary School: A Qualitative Study*. Unpublished Masters Dissertation. University of Malta. https://www.um.edu.mt/library/oar/bitstream/123456789/70835/1/Abela_Marika_2012.pdf. Used with permission of the University of Malta and Marika Abela.

Chapter 11 excerpt taken from p. 571 of Edurne García Iriarte, Patricia O'Brien, Roy McConkey, Marie Wolfe and Siobhain O'Doherty, 2014. Identifying the key concerns of Irish persons with intellectual disability. *Journal of Applied Research in Intellectual Disabilities*, 27(6), pp. 564–575. Used with permission from John Wiley & Sons.

Chapter 12 excerpt taken from the script *Ganesh Versus the Third Reich*, devised by Mark Deans, Marcia Ferguson, Bruce Gladwin, Nicki Holland, Simon Laherty, Sarah Mainwaring, Scott Price, Kate Sulan, Brian Tilley and David Woods. Published in 2013 in the Performance Research Books title *'We're people who do shows'. Back to Back Theatre: Performance, Politics, Visibility*, edited by Helena Grehan and Peter Eckersall. Used with permission of the publisher.

Chapter 13 excerpt taken from Shea MacDonough's letter in E. Wright and C. Edmonds, 2022, 13 May. An 'archaic' law has been removing Australians with disability from the electoral roll 'in droves', advocates say. ABC News. Available from https://www.abc.net.au/news/2022-05-14/disability-voting-laws/101059872. Used with permission from Shea McDonough.

Chapter 14 excerpt taken from p. 49 of Nicki Thorp, Jacqui Stedmon and Helen Lloyd, 2018. 'I carry her in my heart': An exploration of the experience of bereavement for people with learning disability. *British Journal of Learning Disabilities*, 46(1), pp. 45–53. Used with permission from John Wiley & Sons.

Chapter 15 excerpt taken from pp. 163 and 164 of *Summer Brother* by Jaap Robben, translated by David Doherty. Used with permission of the publisher, World Editions. Copyright © 2021, World Editions.

Chapter 16 excerpt taken from a Facebook post by Eva Kittay on 29 February 2024. Used with permission from the author.

1

INTERCONNECTIONS IN THE LIVES OF PERSONS WITH INTELLECTUAL DISABILITY

There is a moment at the end of Kazuo Ishiguro's 2021 novel *Klara and the Sun* when Klara – the Artificial Friend of Josie – states that she could not possibly manage to do what Josie's mum wanted her to do when her daughter was seriously ill: to learn to be Josie and replace her if she were to die. Significantly, Klara does not doubt her own ability to learn how to act exactly like Josie. She is even confident that she could 'learn her heart' (p. 218) with her powerful artificial intelligence. But, what would have stumped Klara, according to her, is that she could not have replaced Josie in the heart of those who loved her:

> But however hard I tried, I believe now there would have remained something beyond my reach. The Mother, Rick, Melania Housekeeper, the Father. I'd never have reached what they felt for Josie in their hearts.
>
> *(Ishiguro 2021, p. 306)*[1]

As a human being who has deep connections with the core people in her life, Josie's self extends beyond the physical limits of her body and is entwined with that of the people closest to her – especially her parents, her friend Rick, and the housekeeper Melania. This image of an unbounded self is possible not because Josie is a character in a work of speculative fiction (after all it is Klara and the other Artificial Friends who are the humanoid machines). It is possible because Josie is a human being, albeit a fictional one.

DOI: 10.4324/9781003561644-1

The relational self

Klara's insight is reflected in various theories which have considered the complexity of the self as not only arising from and residing in the person but as being constituted also of the people with whom one forms intimate connections. Jerome Bruner's 'more "distributed" view of Self' in *Acts of Meaning* (1990, p. 104) provides a particularly useful image that helps us grasp the relational nature of one's own self. Bruner argues that not only is the self not isolated, but that it also takes in the past as well as the present and the wider cultural and historical context, as well as the more immediate one in which one interacts with others. Moreover, Bruner maintains that analyses of this interpersonal self also need 'to attend to the *practices* in which "the meanings of Self" are achieved and put to use' (p. 104, italics in the original). These practices necessarily involve interacting with other persons, and therefore also other – relational – selves.

Through Bruner's concept of the distributed self, Klara's logic can be reversed. If what constitutes Josie is found not only in her heart but also in that of the people closest to her, then the contents of her heart – and their own sense of self – also include her attachments to them. After all, it is with the human Rick and not the humanoid Klara that Josie forms deep-seated ties. In fact, there is a huge contrast between the way Josie blithely tells Klara that she probably would not see her again as she leaves for college and the way that Rick explains to Klara that, even if he and Josie are never physically near each other again, they will remain a part of each other's life and, indeed, of each other's self.

Bruner's argument is closely related to that of Paul Ricoeur in his 1992 book *Oneself as Another*. Helenius (2021) observes that Ricoeur's work is 'concerned about human existence . . . to reveal the capable, meaning actively able, human being' (p. 193). In *Oneself as Another*, Ricoeur delves into the question of the human being through an in-depth and extensive analysis of selfhood, which he relates to ipseity or *ipse*-identity, in order to distinguish it from *idem*-identity or sameness (what he also calls 'character'). The latter is that which enables a person to be recognised as one and the same in different contexts and over time. *Ipse*-identity, on the other hand, is mutable and in a constant process of development. Ricoeur argues that *ipse*-identity can only develop and be discerned through a person's actions (what they say and what they do), and it therefore has dialectic and relational qualities. In fact, the other is brought into Ricoeur's argument time and again, as reflected in the title of his book.

While Ricoeur presents a strong argument against the conflation of *ipse* (selfhood) and *idem* (character), he also acknowledges the way in which the two overlap even because, as he writes, 'this *ipse* announces itself as *idem*' (1992, p. 121). It is, after all, one and the same person that they refer to.

Here, Ricoeur plays with the near-synonyms 'identical' and 'identity'. Thus, *ipse*-identity belongs to the identical person, even as it changes over time. The constancy of the person's identity, Ricoeur argues, is maintained through narrative that links together the different actions, meanings and intentions of that person. When considering the actions and events that are part of a person's narrative, it is not only what happened, where, how and why it happened that are important. The 'who' question is fundamental, thus bringing in the agency of the person and the various actors in their narrative. Narrative also has other notable qualities which, once again, bring in the other. One's narrative cannot mention that one self alone, but necessarily refers to others that one has acted with and upon and whose actions they have reacted to. Likewise, other person's narratives will refer to one's own self. Additionally, one's life narrative is inescapably situated in a wider historical context created by others with social, cultural, political and economic factors impinging on it.

The effects of these macro factors on the individual have been well discussed and theorised through the concept of subjectivity. As Nick Mansfield (2020) states, focusing on the individual as subject serves to 'capture the sense of social and cultural entanglement' and 'the way our immediate daily life is always already caught up in complex political, social and philosophical . . . concerns' (p. 2). These concerns inevitably find their way into this book, but the focus is strategically placed on micro one-to-one encounters, mainly between persons with intellectual disability and non-disabled others: how they relate to each other and impinge on each other's selfhood; and how, through their words and actions, they both shape each other's selfhood and make their own selfhood manifest. What had already happened in a person's immediate and wider context is an integral part of these encounters. After all, one's personal narrative inevitably starts *in media res*. Before self-awareness develops in one's infancy, one's narrative has already started to be recounted by others, as argued, for example, by Judith Butler (2020). Here, too, understanding the person as subject is important. However, whereas I acknowledge that perspectives on subjectivity could usefully complement, nuance and enrich the discussion in this book, a deliberate and strategic decision has been made to focus more exclusively on selfhood. The reason for this decision is that the 'who' question is the central one in my project, warranting attention to be primarily on the person and questions of selfhood, with sociocultural issues being considered in relation to the person.

Wherever one chooses to place the emphasis, bringing the other into the question of selfhood and identity is inevitable. As Ricoeur argues, this inherent connection with the other raises significant ethical issues. The wholesome development of one's *ipse*-identity, or selfhood, necessitates that those persons who have a role in its development behave respectfully towards one. Likewise, one needs to be respectful towards the other and the way one impinges on their selfhood. There is therefore an important ethical principle of reciprocity in operation.

In *Oneself as Another*, Ricoeur addresses this ethical dimension through a discussion of the Golden Rule – doing unto others what you would want others to do unto you. He makes the astute observation that this rule implies an asymmetrical relationship. The one who can apply the Golden Rule in their behaviour and actions is inevitably in a position of being an active agent and the other being a passive recipient of one's actions. There is thus a sense of assuming that it is entirely the agent's responsibility to ensure they are applying the Golden Rule in their relations with others. To use Ricoeur's term, one has 'power-over' (1992, p. 220). If left unchecked, this power-over can descend into the humiliation of and even violence against the other.

But, when that power is exercised in terms of 'power-in-common', 'the members of a historical community . . . exercise in an indivisible manner their desire to live together' (Ricoeur 1992, p. 220), there is reciprocity and egregious behaviour is reined in. One applies the Golden Rule in their behaviour with others, and vice versa. Thus, the other type of power that Ricoeur brings into the picture, the 'power-to-act' (p. 220), is used ethically. One person's power to exercise their agency does not impair the same power in other persons. Rather, the power-to-act is used to nurture each other's agency. Thus, the way in which we affect each other's *ipse*-identity needs to be ethical and reciprocal.

It is this reciprocal dimension in her relationship with Josie that Klara discerns as missing. There is no moral obligation on Josie's part to behave ethically towards Klara because she is humanoid, and therefore not one of the other persons with whom Josie interacts reciprocally, such as her parents, the family's housekeeper and her friend Rick. These persons have Josie inscribed in their hearts as she is inscribed in theirs.

It is also this reciprocal dimension that can be missing in the lives and the selfhood of persons with intellectual disability.

Intellectual disability and the relational self

Ricouer's *Oneself as Another* refers to and builds on the work of Immanuel Kant and John Rawls, among others. However, the distributed relational self, discussed in the previous section, is at odds with the concept of the monadic, rational and self-sufficient self that we have inherited from Kant, among other philosophers. This concept of the self is heavily critiqued in philosophical work about intellectual disability. In her critique of Kant and Rawls, Martha Nussbaum (2006) writes that it 'suggests the idea that the core of our personality is self-sufficient rather than needy, and purely active rather than also passive' (p. 132). Looking at the self as needy, passive and relational can seemingly undermine the idea of it as autonomous, agentic and integral. However, these qualities can be attributed to the discrete as much as to the interconnected self. We can consider the person as being autonomous and also needy; and as acting upon their world and being an agent in their own life, while simultaneously being acted upon by the world, by various structures and by other human beings' agency. It is not a case of either/or; it is a matter of both/and.

When we consider the lived experience of persons with intellectual disability, we can discern the interplay of the intra- and the interpersonal, of the agentic and the dependent, and of the active and the passive. It is the central theme of this book that this interplay is an integral part of the human self in all its complexity, and that looking closely at how persons with intellectual disability experience selfhood can help us better understand them and human experience more generally.

The monadic self oversimplifies what it means to be human and has had a particularly insidious effect on persons with intellectual disability. Having had their personhood and selfhood thrown into doubt made it possible for them to be dehumanised and oppressed – including through institutionalisation, forced sterilisation and even extermination (Snyder and Mitchell 2010), as well as physical, psychological, sexual and financial abuse (Buhagiar and Azzopardi Lane 2022). The activism of persons with intellectual disability, their parents and various allies over the past decades demonstrates their potential and capacity for learning and development and, most importantly, their humanity. This activism stemmed from the pioneering work of the early disability movement, especially in the UK and the US from the 1960s onwards (Campbell and Oliver 1996, Zames Fleischer and Zames 2011).

The most important insights bequeathed to us from this movement have been the social model of disability and the primary importance of disabled persons' perspectives. Thus, there is a distinction between biological impairment and socially created material and conceptual barriers, and a realisation that the barriers play a hugely significant part in creating disability (Thomas 2004). This impact is recognised in anti-discrimination disability legislation, with the most prominent being the United Nations (UN) Convention on the Rights of Persons with Disabilities (2006), which is an important reference point in this book. There is also the realisation that independence and dependence are not mutually exclusive, that one can exercise self-determination while also depending on others (Snow 2010). And there is the overriding principle encapsulated in the slogan 'nothing about us without us' (Charlton 2000). The social model shows us that the lives of persons with intellectual disability are also deeply affected by disabling barriers (Chappell et al. 2001). The daily support that many persons with intellectual disability require and their need for structured learning can be opportunities – rather than stumbling blocks – for growth. 'Nothing about us without us' shows us that the perspectives of persons with intellectual disability are a vital, yet often overlooked, dimension. The situations examined in this book attest to these ideas.

These insights also inform other criticisms of theories of the rational, self-sufficient and monadic self that expose their inadequacy by taking intellectual disability as the test case. In their analysis of the relationship between moral and political philosophy and disability studies, Vehmas and Riddle (2020) largely focus on persons with intellectual disability, discussing how having an intellectual disability does not prevent one from having a good life and reciprocal relationships. Carlson (2010) does much to uncover the misconceptions about intellectual disability found in many philosophical works, especially about personhood. Nussbaum's (2006) critique of Rawls' social contract theory presents a model of human capabilities founded in the basic human experiences that are enjoyed by all, regardless of cognitive ability. These include life, health and bodily integrity; the life of the senses; having reciprocal relationships with others; and having a say in what happens in one's own life.

The starting point for Nussbaum's argument is her own experience of being with persons who were born with severe cognitive impairment. It is, in fact, very important to read closely into the lives of persons with intellectual disability from their own point of view and that of family members and those who support them closely. Vehmas and Riddle (2020) also point out that most people who know persons with intellectual disability would attest to the fact that having such a disability does not in and of itself make one miserable, and that these persons can lead happy lives.

Testimony to the veracity of these statements is provided by the mother of one of the persons Nussbaum writes about, Eva Kittay, philosopher and mother of Sesha, a woman with severe intellectual disability. This book is also heavily influenced by Kittay's work. In *Learning from My Daughter*, Kittay– further developing her work in *Love's Labor* (Kittay 2019a) – asks why dependence is rejected and despised when it is an inevitable part of human experience. She challenges the idea that everyone can achieve self-determination, even when this achievement is understood as reachable with the support and assistance of others. From her position as Sesha's mother, Kittay argues that 'some impairments affect the capacity for self-determination' (2019b, p. 149). Because of her cognitive and physical limitations, Sesha relies entirely on those around her to be willing to find out what gives her joy and to understand her unique mode of communication. The crux of Kittay's argument is that none of these dependencies prevent her daughter from pursuing her personal happiness, since Sesha and all other human beings have properties that are relational and which 'we have only in virtue of the relationships we are in with other human beings' (Kittay 2017, p. 26).

A similar argument is found in Laura Davy's (2015) extension of the feminist concept of relational autonomy to persons with intellectual disability. She argues that the barriers to developing autonomy experienced by persons with intellectual disability – especially those with severe cognitive impairment – do not arise only from that impairment but also from the lack of facilitators for fostering autonomy. The idea of autonomy as something that can be – and needs to be – fostered by others can seem paradoxical. In fact, Davy calls for a reconfiguration of autonomy for it to be understood as 'an ongoing negotiation of the self within interdependent relationships that requires these relationships to be organized in a supportive manner in order to flourish' (p. 146).

These different critiques demonstrate that a narrow understanding of selfhood greatly underestimates the capacities of those who are dependent on various degrees of care and support at certain points in their life or throughout their lifecourse, at certain points or throughout most of their day. It devalues their selfhood, their ability to flourish and – most importantly – their very humanity. Bruner's distributed self and Ricoeur's relational self not only provide a deeper understanding of what it is to have selfhood as a human being. Significantly, these concepts also enable us to appreciate the selfhood of those human beings who have an intellectual disability, even if neither author refers directly to them. Their work, especially Ricoeur's, brings into the discussion the ways in which we mutually impinge on each other's identity, selfhood, subjectivity and personhood, through our relationships with each other.

Intellectual disability and being human

Just like Klara, Sesha has a place in the heart of those who are close to her and they have a place in her heart. The same goes for millions of persons with intellectual disability in the world, regardless of whether their cognitive impairment is assessed as mild, moderate, severe or profound. This book closely studies the particular situation of some persons with intellectual disability and those who share their lives with them and how they impinge on each other's self.

The models of the distributed and the relational self, therefore, apply to them as much as to anyone else. They throw light on how the selfhood of persons with intellectual disability is also co-constructed through the relationships they form throughout their lives. These relationships and how they affect persons with intellectual disability – and how, in turn, the latter affect those they relate with – are unique to each and every person because of different support needs, circumstances and individual qualities. That individual differences count for persons with intellectual disability cannot be overemphasised, and speaking of them as a group is not meant in any way to cast them as homogeneous. However, considering in detail specific aspects of individual experiences, as happens in this book, the negative ideas and misunderstanding that intellectual disability has accrued over centuries mean that persons with intellectual disability also have many experiences in common.

All too often, persons with intellectual disability are dependent on others not only in the practicalities of everyday life but also for the attentive development of their very selfhood. The affirmation is far too often dependent on how others perceive persons with intellectual disability and, consequently, how they interact with them. One story that testifies to this dependence dates from the 1970s. It is told by David Goode, who at the time was doing ethnographic research with people with intellectual disability in the US. As part of his research, Goode visited a long-stay hospital, keeping a tape-recorder on while doing his fieldwork. Goode describes his horrified reaction to the sight of a man with hydrocephalus, whom he perceived as '[a] *huge* head . . . attached to this stunted body. Horrible bedsores covered what appeared for a moment as an almost unreal monstrosity' (1984, p. 230, emphasis in the original). Goode nearly fainted and was rescued by a nurse. Once he had recovered himself, Goode was told by a doctor that the man had blindness, deafness, paralysis and no sign of intelligence. This description led Goode to conclude that '[t]he clinical profile was hopeless . . . the person was as low functioning as one could find' (p. 230). It was only later that Goode could listen on the tape-recorder to what the nurse had said. He found that the nurse had used his name, Johnny, and had described him as 'my special favourite', a young man whose mum she was during the day and who loved rock and roll music and bright lights. The contrast between the two descriptions could not have been sharper. It was the nurse's attitude that responded to Johnny's humanity and helped it flourish, even if to a limited extent.

The achievements of persons with intellectual disability over the past five decades or so are evidence of their potential and capacity for learning and development (Davies et al. 2022). They also attest to the difference that attitudes make, and to the fact that, when others interact with persons with intellectual disability as human beings equal in dignity to them, they are humanised, just like the nurse humanised Johnny. As has already been argued, considering the selfhood and the development of the identity of persons with intellectual disability can tell us much about human identity in general, especially the *ipse*-identity which is the focus of Ricoeur's attention in *Oneself as Another*. However, it is also important to keep in mind those aspects of experience which are of particular relevance for persons with intellectual disability. The chapter in which Goode (1984) recounts his encounter with Johnny nine years earlier is about what he calls 'socially produced, or sociogenic, identity' (p. 231) – that is, the way in which identity emerges in particular situations and through particular interactions. What is problematic for persons with intellectual disability, as Goode argues, is when identity formation 'is not the product of intimate and detailed knowledge of their everyday lives' (p. 232).

When the focus is on cognitive deficit, as with the doctor's description of Johnny in Goode's account, it is very easy to assume a person does not have the potential for personhood. This is especially the case if a person has severe to profound intellectual impairment and additional mobility or sensory impairments or other complex dependency needs. It is also easy to make the next logical step and assume that such persons do not have a claim to a fully human status. Such arguments are made by John McMahan (2003) and Peter Singer (2010), who compare the intellectual abilities of persons with severe intellectual impairment with some animal species to argue in favour of animal rights. The arguments Nussbaum, Goode and Kittay (and those of many others who – like them – write and speak of persons with intellectual disability whom they have got to know well) are very important not only because they counter such dehumanising arguments and attitudes. They are also important because they serve as a voice, albeit indirectly, for persons who cannot articulate their perspectives directly, precisely because of the severe nature of their intellectual impairment.

These arguments rescue the reciprocity in the relationships that persons with intellectual disability enjoy. This reciprocity, as seen in Klara's reasoning and in Bruner's and Ricoeur's theories, has a vital role in the development of identity and selfhood. That it can be compromised especially when there are complex dependency needs that arise from mental and physical impairments also highlights the role of embodiment in identity formation. Not only does this formation occur in specific historical contexts, as discussed earlier, but it also has an embodied element to it, as argued by Ricoeur, echoing Merleau-Ponty's phenomenological analyses. When a person's embodiment is very far from what is considered typical, as in the case of Johnny and Sesha for example, this formation can easily be undermined before it has even begun.

The cognitive limitations experienced by persons with intellectual disability may impede – to various extents –their ability to carry out tasks that adults are typically expected to execute unassisted. Their dependence on others means that their developmental trajectory is not only affected by their impairments but also by the available support. This support, in turn, depends on the willingness and ability of others to provide it. At a more fundamental level, it depends on taking a support-based, rather than a deficit-based, approach.

Such an approach is advocated in the most recent edition of the manual on intellectual disability of the American Association on Intellectual and Developmental Disabilities (AAIDD) (Schalock et al. 2021). That the AAIDD has adopted a position which does not stop at the assessment of intellectual functioning and adaptive behaviour but also embraces the importance of contextual and cultural factors, as well as the individual's strengths and support needs, is noteworthy. It reflects an affirmative attitude towards persons with intellectual disability and a rejection of the negative ideas that have caused so many to lead abject lives. Vestiges of these ideas still exist and still affect many persons with intellectual disability. Were this not the case, there would surely be no need to continue advocating for significant improvements in their lives. Delving into the lives of persons with intellectual disability, consequently, does not only require a close examination of how their selfhood is intertwined with those of the persons they interact with. This delving also needs to take in the type of relationships that persons with intellectual disability experience with others, and others with them.

Understanding the lived experience of persons with intellectual disability

How then can one set about seeking an understanding of the lived experience of persons with intellectual disability? This question begs others, among them:

Whose perspective(s) should be used to reach an understanding?
When can we know that we have reached an adequate understanding?
What can possible answers to these questions tell us about persons with intellectual disability as fellow human beings and, therefore, about humanity itself?

These are the questions that are addressed in the following chapters, without any expectation of reaching full and definitive answers, but with the aim of providing pointers to such answers in the concluding chapter, which also returns to the title of this book. This section fleshes out the methodological framework on which the chapters are based.

Here, I turn to phenomenology, particularly as it is used in the social sciences. In philosophy, the phenomenological tradition has embraced different approaches, such as Husserl's transcendental phenomenology, Heidegger's hermeneutics and Merleau-Ponty's body-subject. A recent approach is that of critical phenomenology, which factors in 'how contingent historical and social structures also shape our experience . . . in what we might call a quasi-transcendental way' (Weiss et al. 2020, p. 21).

Applied to disability, critical phenomenology takes in the lived experience of impairment and functional limitations, and of the structural and cultural barriers encountered by those who have impairments. Critical phenomenology has been used in disability studies, most notably to investigate the lived experience of bodily impairments and neurodiversity, such as in the 2020 special issue of *Puncta: Journal of Critical Phenomenology* on illness, madness and disability. In this issue, Abrams (2020) argues that critical phenomenology builds on the phenomenological tradition by factoring in cultural and attitudinal factors towards disability. Additionally, the same issue carries discussions on the intersections of studies of disability and chronic illness and critical phenomenology by Jacobson (2020), who brings the role of the space that an individual inhabits into the consideration of their lived experience, and by Valentine (2020), who focuses on intersubjectivity as part of the lived experience.

No specific research methodology based on critical phenomenology has yet been developed. For my methodology, I turn to Max Van Manen. Although his work is situated within the classical phenomenological tradition, there is scope for extending it to critical phenomenology. In the Introduction to *Researching Lived Experience*, Van Manen (2016a) states that doing phenomenological research 'is always to question the way we experience the world, to want to know the world in which we live as human beings' (p. 5). This world is obviously not just the physical object that we call planet Earth. It is also the particular historical, sociocultural and interpersonal contexts that we inhabit.

Furthermore, in *Phenomenology of Practice*, Van Manen describes phenomenological inquiry as thinking about 'the prereflective or prepredicative experience' through 'musing, reflective questioning, and being obsessed with sources and meanings of lived meaning' (2016b, p. 26). Taking time out to talk or write about a past experience entails a degree of reflection, even if at a very basic level. Van Manen provides examples of writings where the recollection of a past experience is described in details which are as objective as possible; and this is perhaps the most feasible way to gain access to the basic experience on which a phenomenological gaze is then cast. Verbal accounts can also be created in research interviews, among other methods of the social sciences. Whichever method is used, there is always a deferral between the actual occurrence of an experience and its recounting.

Van Manen further argues that, while language is cognitive, it is used to understand experience, which is both cognitive and pathic. The phenomenological project, therefore, has inherent limitations. However, even if the moment can only be grasped after the fact and partially so, there is still much that can be profitably reflected upon to gain insight and understanding. In this manner, we can seek to return to 'the things themselves', to use Husserl's often quoted phrase.

The thing being returned to here is the lived experience of people with intellectual disability. In line with Van Manen's methodology, the actual experiences that are submitted to phenomenological analysis are mostly common, everyday experiences, which are also lived through by persons with intellectual disability. Seeking an understanding of their lived experience can address the 'what is it like?' question that Van Manen says is asked in phenomenology; in this case the question being 'what is it like to be a person with intellectual disability in the world?'

As discussed above, and as shown by the extensive research carried out with people with intellectual disability around the world (some of which is discussed or cited in this book), the contexts that persons with intellectual disability live in are far from neutral. Socially constructed disabling barriers – material and attitudinal, tangible and intangible – form a significant part of their lifeworld. On the other hand, since, as Van Manen explains, phenomenology's 'method aims at uncovering and seeing through the presumptions and suppositions that shape our understanding of the world and understanding of life' (2016b, p. 54), taking sociocultural factors on board as part of the prereflective experience can be seen as running counter to phenomenology.

The question then has to be asked about whether the material and attitudinal barriers encountered by persons with intellectual disability in their lives are part of the original experience – of 'the primal concreteness of lived reality' (Van Manen 2016b, p. 41) – or part of the conceptual scaffolding through which we can analyse that experience. Most human experiences are played out in interactions with other human beings. These interactions, as seen above, directly impinge on one's self. How one is perceived and related to by others will therefore be part of these experiences and of the self. When having a specific attribute – such as a cognitive impairment – presents a high risk of being related to not as an equal but as someone who is lacking traits associated with being human, how one is perceived is very likely to have significant repercussions on how one is related to and how one experiences the world.

If the phenomenological gaze entails suspending one's natural attitude by bracketing one's assumptions and presuppositions through the epoché, these considerations prompt us to question what we should bracket when it comes to analysing the lived experience of persons with intellectual disability. Is it the assumption that they are little more than the sum of their impairments, as Johnny's doctor described him to Goode? Or is it the assumption that they have human potential which may need direct input from those around them to emerge, as Johnny's nurse did? These two questions do not present a choice between bracketing and not bracketing. They present a choice between recognising the humanity of persons with intellectual disability in its fullness and not recognising it. When the balance of the experiences of persons with intellectual disability around the world and across the centuries tilts towards negativity and dehumanisation, going for the (re)humanising option is the only feasible choice.

When the lifeworld of a person is directly mediated by factors that are outside their control and which can have significant beneficial or deleterious effects on it, when other people's attitudes – and therefore one's relationship with them – are a crucial factor in the person's lived experience, these factors need to be considered as part of the prereflective primal experience that is the subject of phenomenological investigation. Hence the relevance of critical phenomenology.

Considering the experiences of persons with intellectual disability as they are lived in relation to others is not only important but, I argue, inevitable. This is because intellectual disability always already has a social as well as a biological component. Persons with intellectual disability are who they are not only because they have their individual differences as human beings, not only because of their impairments and how they affect their lives, but also because the immediate environment in which that development has taken place and the wider sociocultural context have dramatic effects on them. Like everyone, they live in an intentional world. In their case, the intentionality directed at them comprises how those interacting with them perceive persons with intellectual disability. Taking a close look at how various factors are enmeshed in their lives can bring out very clearly the way that the relational self is constructed and how it works. Consequently, analysing the lived experience of persons with intellectual disability needs to bring relations and interactions with others on board. And if these relations contribute to the construction of the distributed and relational self, then the study of that lived experience is closely aligned with a study of the self.

Furthermore, if the self of each and every human being is relational, then, as discussed earlier, what emerges from a study of the lives of persons with intellectual disability can help us better understand the human self. The cover photograph of Kittay's *Learning from My Daughter* is a close-up of the author and her daughter holding hands. The author photo on the dust jacket also shows the two together. Mother and daughter are walking in a park, Sesha in a wheelchair, Eva beside her. They are holding hands and looking at each other with what can only be described as smiles of joy. It is significant that Eva Kittay did not choose a photograph of herself on her own for this book. The choice is a very appropriate one, since it highlights how closely related to each other the two of them are and how intertwined their selves are.

Book structure

Van Manen (2016a, 2016b) argues that researching lived experience entails analyses of detailed description of that experience, often referred to as 'thick' descriptions in the social sciences. This type of description affords a close look at specific aspects of life. The experience under scrutiny in this book – that of people with intellectual disability – is vast and only certain aspects of it could be considered within the scope of the book. In each of the next 14 chapters, a specific scene in the life of a person with intellectual disability is analysed. The scenes are presented in very short excerpts taken from already published qualitative research, and also from an unpublished dissertation, an autobiography, a letter, a podcast interview, a short video, a playscript, a photograph, a novel and a poem. This variety results from a deliberate choice to use different types of texts in order to highlight how, as Van Manen (2016b) argues, meaning can be found in different texts, including fiction.

The chapter titles are aimed at capturing the single most salient aspect of each scene, thus providing the main focus for that chapter. The excerpts that are analysed have been carefully chosen to represent encounters between persons with intellectual disability and non-disabled others that allow for layers of interpretation to be elicited. They represent a variety of settings. Three of the scenes take place in mainstream schools: in Chapter 2, Josephine is in the school gym; in Chapter 4, adolescent students go on a school outing; and in Chapter 10, Leon has a meltdown in the school corridor. Chapter 3 considers Noli's supported employment and Chapter 7 focuses on Lauren's acting career. Leisure activities set the scenes for Chapter 6 (Giovanni going to the carnival), Chapter 8 (organising a social life for persons with profound intellectual and multiple disabilities) and Chapter 11 (someone going to the bar). Chapter 5 considers Eve's family photo, Chapter 9 Noelle's poem on friendship, Chapter 12 Brian's idea for a play chapter, Chapter 13 Shea being able to vote, Chapter 14 Rachel mourning her grandfather and, finally, in Chapter 15 Lucien's experience with institutionalisation. The excerpts have also been chosen to present a variety of perspectives – those of persons with intellectual disability, of family members and of those who work with them. Some of the scenes depicted provide examples of inclusion and affirmative relationships, while others represent the opposite or a mixture of both. There is no particular order to these chapters and they can be read independently of each other.

Using short excerpts allows for an in-depth analysis of the situation depicted, of musing, reflecting and obsessing on the multiple layers of meaning in each scene, to paraphrase Van Manen. Each analysis brings in references to other relevant details from the publication from which the excerpt is taken, as well as to the relevant literature, in order to enable a comprehensive understanding. Different aspects of life are considered, and each chapter's discussion also takes in the relevant disabling barriers and enabling factors that persons with intellectual disability experience. As argued earlier, these factors are a part of their lived experience and impinge directly on their sense of self. They are gradually uncovered through a minute analysis of each scene and its context.

Delving deeply into each excerpt elicits the intricate connections established in the lives of persons with intellectual disability, the relationships they have with people in their lives and the effect that these connections and relationships have on their selfhood. Additionally, the factors that impinge on the life experiences of each person with intellectual disability and how they are interlinked are considered, including through referring to the relevant literature. What the analyses of the different scenes have in common is the realisation that what lies at the heart of the lifeworld of persons with intellectual disability is how they are perceived and how they are related to.

This theme is picked up in the analysis in the final chapter, which starts with an excerpt from a Facebook post by Eva Kittay as a reference point to explore how the selfhood of each person with intellectual disability is distributed rather than discrete, relational rather than monadic. It is in this manner that looking at the lives of persons with intellectual disability can teach us much about human experience. At the same time, the particular lived experience of persons with intellectual disability and how it affects their own selfhood needs to be emphasised, dependent as they are on their relationships with others in so many aspects of their daily lives and the degree of reciprocity in these relationships. The analysis thus also throws light on how we can make the lives of persons with intellectual disability better by being attentive to how we relate to them.

Note

1 Excerpt taken from *Klara and the Sun* by Kazuo Ishiguro. Published by Faber & Faber, 2021. Copyright © Kazuo Ishiguro. Reproduced by permission of the author c/o Rogers, Coleridge & White Ltd., 20 Powis Mews, London W11 1JN.

2

JOSEPHINE KEEPS HER SOCKS ON IN THE SCHOOL GYM

> One of Josephine's PE [physical education] lessons provides a good example of this. When they were doing activities in the gym she was quite upset that some of the children had laughed at her feet, because she has quite unusual feet where her toes are fused. I contacted the school about this and was told that it wasn't a problem, in future in PE lessons she could just keep her socks on. Clearly the problem was just Josephine and not that they had to deal with it at all. This was very much how the school viewed her: she was the problem and there was nothing wrong with the way they were organised, or with the school culture.
>
> Tsokova and Tarr (2012, p. 31)[1]

This quotation is taken from the joint narrative by Josephine and her mother Carol about the daughter's experiences in the different schools she attended in her native UK, presented in Tsokova and Tarr's (2012) book *Diverse Perspectives on Inclusive School Communities*. The 'this' that Carol mentions in the first sentence is what she had just described as the school's lack of knowledge about how to make adaptations to include Josephine.

Like the curate's egg, Josephine's inclusion in this school can be said to have been good in parts. It worked insofar as she was a student with disability in her local mainstream secondary school, with a teaching assistant to support her. But it seems that this was where adjustments for her inclusion tended to stop. Carol chooses the incident in the gym as a manifestation of the limited inclusion enjoyed by Josephine in this particular school, which she later contrasts with a more successful instance of inclusion.

In this excerpt, we find Josephine doing a PE lesson with her classmates in the gym. They are barefoot. Josephine has Apert syndrome, which causes

DOI: 10.4324/9781003561644-2

cognitive as well as physical impairment, including anomalies in the feet. It is Josephine's unseparated toes that become the focus of the story once she takes her socks off.

Earlier, Carol had explained how other people's reactions to her daughter's physical differences have created obstacles for her throughout her life and the profound influence they have had on her, to the extent that 'learning how to relate to people became problematic because she could not predict what people's reactions would be' (Tsokova and Tarr 2012, p. 30). When Josephine bared her feet in the gym along with her classmates, another adverse reaction from others was added to Josephine's lived experience.

For Josephine, her feet are as much a part of her as the rest of her body, and an integral part of how she presents herself to the world. In that moment when some children laughed, Josephine's feet became her and she became her feet, fused toes and all. It came as no consolation that some, but not all, children laughed, and that it was her feet they laughed at. The attention drawn to her feet and the subsequent laughter served as a reminder that she had only been accepted in her school to a certain degree. Any attempts at pushing the boundaries further than the limits set by the school were resisted. This is not to say that Josephine was deliberately pushing preset boundaries. After all, all she did was remove her socks to be barefoot like her classmates. But the very action that she undertook to be like them served as yet another reminder of how unlike them she was considered to be. This reminder of difference was only exacerbated by the solution proffered by the school – that of hiding her additional difference with socks.

The fact that this incident happened as Josephine was growing up is significant. Because of her condition, Josephine would not have been expected to follow the same developmental trajectory as her non-disabled peers. But there is also her developing sense of self to consider. As mentioned above, Josephine's unusual appearance – the face and body with which she presents herself to the world and to other people – affects her relationship with others, and has done since she was a baby. Her self has therefore emerged in a world and through relationships that have not always been benign in their effect on her. There are also interactions which have not always been open to receiving her as she is, on her own terms. The contrast between Josephine's stockinged feet and the bare feet of her classmates becomes symbolic of the barriers she faces in building deep and meaningful relationships with the people in her life, barriers that her typically developing classmates are unlikely to face.

But at least Josephine was with other children and could relate to them and their educators, even if not unconditionally. Her being in the gym that day when she was laughed at by some children did not happen by chance. A number of factors, of different origins, preceded it. Among these we can identify: the genetic anomaly that caused Josephine's Apert syndrome; the long history of separating persons with disabilities from the mainstream of society (Mansell and Ericsson 1996) and children with disabilities from the mainstream of education (Cardona 2011); the eventual affirmation of the latter's right to be educated alongside their non-disabled peers (UNESCO 1994); and the various policies and practices emanating from the recognition of this right. These include legislation specific to inclusive education in various countries, with the US leading the way with the impact that the Americans with Disabilities Act had in 1990 on the Individuals with Disabilities Education Act of 1975 (Bérubé 2016), and Article 24 of the Convention on the Rights of Persons with Disabilities (2006) (CRPD), which stipulates the right to inclusive education.

These factors operate at different levels: from supranational legislation and national laws and the provision of services and resourcing by governments; to the actual placement of students with intellectual or other disabilities in mainstream school; through to the one-to-one interactions that these students have with their classmates and educators, and the relationships that develop from these micro interactions. All of these factors, which led to that moment in the gym, cannot be laid out neatly in linear fashion. But they can be seen as a set of actions and reactions that provide its context. They can also be seen as coming together at the moment that Josephine had to show her fused toes, when her classmates looked at them and some of them laughed.

The laughter indicates a much wider context to consider. This is the cultural perception of disability, especially intellectual disability, which the children who laughed had unwittingly received and which influenced their reaction to Josephine's unusual appearance. This culture has largely been negative, especially with the onset of institutionalisation in many countries from the nineteenth century onwards. As Jarrett (2020) observes, this period marks a shift in attitudes towards persons with intellectual disability from people whose care was the responsibility of the communities to which they belonged to people who needed to be placed in institutions and under medical care, away from the communities that they were no longer seen as belonging to.

Inclusive education is an important tool in undoing the harm done by institutionalisation, documented by Snyder and Mitchell (2010) among many others. It is informed by the principle of community inclusion, which imbues the CRPD. It also works to achieve the aim of community inclusion. Furthermore, it is 'in the communities in which they [persons with disabilities] live' (Article 24.2(b)) that inclusive education needs to take place and, therefore, also in daily practices and interactions.

That moment when Josephine's bared feet provoked laughter led to further actions and reactions. As noted earlier, the laughter was enough for this incident to create another notch in Josephine's memory of the negative experiences that arise because of the way she presents herself to others and the way that others react to this presentation. Additionally, it became emblematic of what was not going well at the school that Josephine was attending at the time, in terms of her inclusion. As Carol observes, for the school the solution was not to fight against attitudes that excluded but to hide that which brought such attitudes to the fore. The solution is a pseudo-solution, one that perpetuates the difficulties that it purports to solve.

Thus, what the school did or did not do, especially the reaction of the staff members concerned, takes on a particular significance. Through their reply and their pseudo-solution, these educators indirectly acknowledged the problematic nature of the reaction of the children who laughed at Josephine's toes. But, for them, the locus of the problem was not the way that some of the children seemed to have imbibed an attitude of laughing at some aspects of physical difference. The locus, rather, was Josephine's fused toes, and the problem was solvable by asking her to keep her socks on.

Through the school's solution, Josephine is asked to fit into a norm which is pre-established even if it is not explicitly articulated. The partial acceptance of Josephine's atypical embodiment becomes a stand-in for the manifold ways in which the acceptance of her own self in this school is only partial. For the educators concerned, Josephine fitting in meant hiding her physical difference as much as possible. For Carol and her daughter, it meant Josephine going sockless like the others. Judging from various online postings on the subject, taking one's socks off in the school gym can be an issue for some children. To take just two examples, on the Quora (2021) forum a student asked if they could keep their socks on in the school gym, even if the teacher asks everyone to take their socks off, because 'there was a time where they want to touch my feet and I hated it'. The UK-based *Metro* online newspaper reports about a school that made children do their PE lessons barefoot unless they had gym shoes with white soles, so that they did not ruin the newly laid expensive floor (King 2021).

In these and similar examples, the issue is the reverse of the one encountered by Josephine since they concern students who wanted to keep their socks on. But what these situations have in common is a focus on the problems that arise when schoolchildren, or any other group of human beings, are all expected to follow the same rule.

There were also instances of inclusion for Josephine. Carol recounts, for example, how in another school a Maths teacher took the time to speak with Josephine about what would help her be included during her lessons, rather than just leaving her to work only with her teaching assistant. Carol observes that '[t]he key difference was that she would talk to Josephine about what she needed and checked with her if she could see the board' (Tsokova and Tarr 2012, p. 33).

In her own narrative, Josephine describes how she felt excluded to a higher degree in secondary school, compared to her experience in other schools. But, even when it did happen, inclusion only occurred in pockets for Josephine, and the incident with her sockless feet in the gym becomes emblematic of the majority of experiences recounted by Josephine and her mother in Tsokova and Tarr's book.

Judging from the many reports and studies about inclusive education that have been published, the incident can indeed be taken as being representative of such attitudes not just in Josephine's case but more widely. In their General Comment on Article 24 of the CRPD (Education), the Committee on the Rights of Persons with Disabilities (2016) laments the barriers that still exist despite the right to 'inclusive, quality and equitable education' (p. 1) being recognised in the CRPD as well as in the United Nations (UN) Sustainable Development Goals (SDGs). As the Committee points out, having inclusive education entails current educational systems undergoing transformational change. Among the barriers identified by the Committee are '[l]ack of knowledge . . . lack of outreach to all parents; and lack of appropriate responses to support requirements' (2016, p. 2), all of which apply to the incident with Josephine's socks in the gym. The Committee then discusses in detail the steps needed to be taken to make education truly inclusive, steps that Josephine's former secondary school and all other educational institutions would do well to pay heed to.

Evidence of the patchy nature of the implementation of inclusive education is found in various reports and research papers. For example, Reiser's 2012 report on the implementation of inclusive education in the British Commonwealth notes that no single developed or developing country had implemented a fully inclusive education system. Similar situations are reported in various European countries and in the United States by the contributors to Dovigo's (2017) *Special Educational Needs and Inclusive Practices: An International Perspective*.

Loreman (2014) identifies the need for an education system that provides a climate which welcomes difference and supports innovation – for inclusive school and classroom practices, collaboration within and among schools and with the families of children with disabilities, and providing individualised support for these children. These needs are echoed in more recent reports. The UN Special Rapporteur on Disability (2021) notes the lack of inclusive educational systems. Likewise, the Country Policy Review and Analysis by the European Agency for Special Needs and Inclusive Education (EASNIE 2021) provides specific recommendations for putting in place the necessary policies to address the shortcomings related to inclusion identified in an analysis of the relevant policies of the Agency's 21 member countries.

Therefore, while legislation and policies are fundamental to putting into place an inclusive education system, inclusion actually happening is ultimately dependent on what the day-to-day interactions between children with disabilities and their educators are like, and on how these interactions are impinged upon by what goes on within the wider education system. In her narrative, Carol refers to low expectations for Josephine from her primary school teachers which led to her underachieving, both academically and socially. In fact, when it comes to students with intellectual disability, their inclusion tends to be more precarious than that for students with physical or sensory impairments. In their systematic review of research about inclusive education, Van Mieghem et al. (2020) note that teachers, parents and non-disabled children tend to have more negative attitudes towards the former than the latter. They also report on students with severe intellectual disability being more likely to experience bullying. The inclusion, or lack thereof, of students with intellectual disability is also addressed in Inclusion International's 2018 pamphlet that responds to the most common myths and misconceptions about inclusive education for students with intellectual disability, including the mistaken idea that inclusion may work for students with other types of disability but not for those who have cognitive impairment.

Ultimately, the effectiveness of inclusive education for children with intellectual disability, as for other children who are at risk of exclusion, depends on a range of micro to macro factors. At one end, there needs to be an in-depth understanding across the board of what inclusion truly means and the transformation needed to bring it about. At the other end, it comes down to the nature of the daily interactions between children with intellectual disability and their educators. But these two distinct ends of the inclusion continuum – and all legislation, policies, measures and actions that are located between them – can also be seen as different facets of inclusion. Their effectiveness can only ever be known by understanding how each and every child experiences inclusion.

In the discussion of the scene presented in the opening excerpt, Josephine's bared fused toes become a synecdoche for her negative experiences of being included at school, a manifestation of both her physical and cognitive difference. Most of the time, her feet are kept hidden from view by socks and shoes. The attention drawn to them the moment she bared them was both unwelcome and unwelcoming as it served as a reminder that Josephine's inclusion was only partial and that, despite the requirements for schools to change and adapt to become fully inclusive for each and every child, the onus is still largely on children with disabilities to conform to educational systems. Students with intellectual disability – of all ages – are hit particularly hard by this need to conform because of the difficulties they encounter in keeping up with the curriculum being followed by their peers.

The hiding from view of Josephine's bared feet reminds us that children with disabilities will continue to be largely hidden from view in mainstream schools unless the needed transformation is achieved. It also reminds us that educational inclusion – or exclusion – has a direct impact on each and every child with disability as they are growing up and establishing their own place in the world. Inclusive education is not only about enabling persons with disabilities to achieve their potential alongside their peers, to have their rights respected and to be provided with the support and reasonable accommodation that they need. It is also about attending to person-to-person interactions and ensuring that those who do not have an intellectual disability approach these interactions with an open mind to accept those who do just as they are.

Josephine's socks are also symbolic of the way in which invisible barriers can be raised to fully accepting persons with intellectual disability as they are and to make them feel fully accepted. Such barriers may be created inadvertently, and even through good intentions. This seems to be the case for Josephine's educators, which means that it is all the more important to be attentive to interpersonal relations with persons with intellectual disability, from when they are children. Understanding the impact that words and actions – however well meant – can have on them from their own point of view is vital because it is not just their rights and their wellbeing that are affected through their interactions with others, but their very self.

Note

1 Excerpt taken from p. 31 of Diana Tsokova and Jane Tarr, 2012. *Diverse Perspectives on Inclusive School Communities*. Taylor & Francis. Used with permission of Taylor & Francis.

3

NOLI PACKS ORANGES AT THE MARKET

> Noli: Ana is my job coach. She always supports me. She helps me to be responsible. She helps my family not to be afraid. I talk to Ana about the job. Ana helps me to learn how to handle money. I trust her a lot. She takes me to workshops, courses. I am happy with her.
>
> Inclusion Europe (2020b)[1]

This excerpt is from one of six videos produced for the 'My Talents For Diversity' (MTFD) project, led by Inclusion Europe, Plena Inclusión (Spain), EVPIT (Estonia) and Antwerp Management School (Belgium). The aim of the project is '*to promote diversity management amongst private and public employers*' (Inclusion Europe 2020a, italics in the original).

Manuela (known as Noli) is one of the persons with intellectual disability featuring in the videos. Her story very neatly encapsulates the many and varied aspects of the experience of persons with intellectual disability in their efforts to secure and maintain employment. The excerpt above highlights the importance of supportive interpersonal relationships at work. These types of relationships, and the individualised support arrangements from which they arise, are particularly important for persons with intellectual disability, as shown in Noli's video. They are also arrangements and relationships which reflect more general practices that can make workplaces more equitable, in line with the requirements of Article 27 (Work and Employment) of the UN Convention on the Rights of Persons with Disabilities (2006).

Noli works on a stall in a market in Tenerife, and her main job is to prepare bags of fruits and vegetables to be sold. Ana, her job coach, explains how a job was customised for Noli, based on her skills, what she enjoys

DOI: 10.4324/9781003561644-3

doing, and what Hugo, her employer, needed to get done. The disability services and support organisation Evenbreak (2022) explains how job carving is used to identify tasks that an individual with disability can do and which also meet the needs of the employer who will be recruiting that individual. This approach reverses the employment process, which usually starts with a call for vacancies for someone to work according to a predetermined job description (Nietupski and Hamre-Nietupski 2000). In Noli's case, a task was identified that Hugo, the stall owner, used to have to do after the market had closed. Thanks to Noli, that job is now done during the day.

The support needs of individuals with intellectual disability in the workplace can go beyond the practical side of being shown how to do a job. In fact, from Noli's comments about her job coach, we gather that Ana has also become her confidante. Noli talks to Ana, and the latter supports her in her personal development as well – Noli mentions how Ana helps her be responsible and handle money as well as by finding opportunities for her to continue learning through workshops and courses.

Noli's testimony indicates a dependence on the job coach that goes beyond what is ordinarily expected of someone working in open employment. Employment is one of the chief markers of adulthood. It is both a right and a duty. Adults have the right to expect having employment opportunities – in line with the UN Universal Declaration of Human Rights (1948) – at the same time as they are expected to be in employment. Committing oneself to a paid job means that one is (or at least is striving to be) financially independent while contributing to society and to the economy. It also means that a person divests themselves of the dependence on others that is a marker of childhood and of old age. Like the human being in the Sphinx's riddle, adults are expected to be able to walk on their own two feet, without the need to resort to crawling on all fours or using a walking stick, metaphorical or otherwise.

Transposing the Sphinx's riddle to the world of work thus highlights how employees are expected to carry out their job unaided. Noli's experiences – and those of other persons with intellectual disability who need support in employment – challenge these expectations (Pleven and Callus 2017). Jessie Nelson's film *I Am Sam* (2001) also provides a confounding portrayal of the eponymous character, Sam, who has an intellectual disability. While the plot upholds Sam's right to be a father to Lucy and not have her taken away from him, it also shows his limitations – including in the way he messes up when he gets a promotion from clearing tables to serving customers from behind the bar. It is a fact that Sam is capable of working, living in his own apartment and using his resourcefulness to get his daughter back from the foster parents that the state has entrusted her to. It is also a fact that he needs support to raise his daughter, that his reading age is that of a seven-year old and that there are only certain tasks he can carry out at work. But the film shows how the response to these facts is not to deny Sam and Lucy the chance to grow together, thus also shaping each other's self, but to ensure that Sam has the support he requires to ensure that Lucy's childhood needs are catered for.

The importance of this support emerges from many studies into the factors that promote or block the employment of persons with intellectual disability. These studies include Australian ones reviewed by Meltzer et al. (2020), those reviewed by Cheng et al. (2018), mostly carried out in the USA, and studies from various countries reviewed by Ellenkamp et al. (2016). Vlachou et al. (2021) discuss the need for emotional support for persons with intellectual disability in Greece in the initial stages of their employment. Furthermore, in Garrels and Sigstad's (2019) research on employment experiences of Norwegian persons with intellectual disability, various participants talk about the help they have received. Among others, Robert describes how he did not 'understand anything' but now has 'everything under control' and how proud he is of what he has learnt (pp. 254–255); Emily explains about the problem she had when she had 'to cook porridge, and at the same time peel eggs, and then the porridge got burned' (p. 255); and Ahmed explains how he needs to be in sheltered employment before he can consider having 'a real job' where he would be expected 'to be on time and work properly' (p. 256), which he was not confident on being able to achieve at the time of the interview.

Garrels and Sigstad (2019) describe Ahmed's explanation as 'candid' (p. 256). In fact, Robert, Emily, Ahmed and Noli can all be described as being candid about their support needs. They experience these needs as an integral part of their life, and do not see them as running counter to their employability. Supported employment is in fact a well-established practice not only for persons with intellectual disability but also for other persons for whom entering open employment without support is a daunting prospect (SAMSHA 2012). The need for support from others is part of who they are. Like many other disabled people, they do not see this need as incompatible with being independent because independence is understood as doing things on your own terms – with support where necessary – rather than simply doing things on your own (Morris 1993). Noli's account demonstrates how the provision of support extends into other aspects of life for her as well. She shows herself to be dependent on Ana to learn money management and to continue with her development through furthering her education. Ana is also spoken of by Noli as someone who offers her ongoing support and someone that she can talk to about her job.

The words in the opening excerpt that contradict expectations of adulthood most directly are 'she helps me to be responsible'. Being responsible for oneself can be taken as the ultimate marker of adulthood and the expectation of independence that comes with it. Being responsible for oneself means that one is 'capable of fulfilling an obligation or duty', as the *Oxford English Dictionary* tells us. It is therefore something that is envisaged to be done on one's own because, the moment one is supported to do something, the responsibility for it is shared. Not only that; responsibility also means being able to be in charge of something and/or of other people, of being responsible for what they do. Needing help to be responsible, therefore, sounds highly contradictory.

In fact, supported employment, such as that provided for Noli, does not just reverse the recruitment process. It also challenges the logic of employment and how it is conceptualised. Noli articulates this challenge really well in the video, not least in the way she comes across as being really proud of her work and happy doing it. Her work entails preparing pre-weighed bags of oranges and potatoes (among other fruit and vegetables), that Hugo then sells. This saves the latter precious time while the market is open and also afterwards. Therefore, the job that has been carved out for Noli addresses an actual need for the smooth running of Hugo's market stall. From the parts in the video where we see Noli at work, we can conclude that she has become adept at performing the tasks related to her job. Noli's contribution filled a gap in the running of the stall. She has even extended her job, and provides added value to it by helping older customers carry their shopping to their cars.

Simultaneously, Noli continues to experience the need for support on a personal level in life domains that most employees are assumed to have achieved full independence. What is striking in the video as a whole and in the excerpt that this chapter focuses on is that these two aspects – Noli's successful inclusion in the labour market and her continuing need for support from her job coach – do not come across as contradictory. Rather than the latter nullifying the former, the two are complementary facets of Noli's employment and her life.

Additionally, the visual content of the video presents Noli as an employee like any other. She and Hugo exchange a peck on the cheek as they greet each other when Noli arrives. We watch her carrying out the actual task of putting oranges in bags, weighing them, adjusting the amount of fruit to go into a bag according to the desired weight, discussing with Hugo and engaging with older customers to help them with their shopping.

It is not only what Noli says and how she is presented that is remarkable. The way she speaks, with confidence and with a smile on her face, is also noteworthy. She does not change tone between when she speaks about her ambition to work, the job that she does and her need for support from Ana. All these aspects are spoken about by Noli with the same level of self-assurance. It is from this position of self-confidence that Noli speaks openly about the ways that Ana provides her with support. She also states how happy she is with Ana's presence in her life.

The cohesive manner in which Noli talks about both her employment-related abilities and her support needs is reflected as well in the way she is presented and spoken about by Ana and Hugo. The disability motifs that one often finds in the media – especially those of someone being able to do something 'despite their disability' (critiqued by Bendukurthi and Raman 2020, among others) and those inviting wonder at the supposedly extraordinary achievements of disabled people (Titchkovsky 2020) – are absent in Noli's video and in the others in the same project. Noli is both capable *and* in need of support. What she has achieved employment-wise she has not accomplished alone. In narratives such as those critiqued by Bendukurthi and Raman and Titchkovsky, there is rarely any mention of the support that disabled people often depend on to gain their achievements. On the contrary, Noli's dependence on others is presented alongside her capabilities, and it is spoken of matter-of-factly.

Consequently, highlighting the abilities of persons with intellectual disability – in this case in relation to employment – and their dependency needs are not contradictory but complementary. It is narratives of someone achieving 'despite their disability' and those that contrast a person's physical or mental impairments with their accomplishments that create a dichotomy. Noli's video shows clearly how this dichotomy is false.

From the complementarity of the provision of support and of job opportunities in the open labour market arises a relationship of reciprocity between Noli and Hugo, between persons with intellectual disability and their employers. The reciprocity goes beyond the good relationship between the two. It is also there because, as Hugo says, employing Noli has been 'both economically and emotionally rewarding'.

Achieving supported employment requires state funding, as Meltzer et al. (2020) mention. This funding covers the job coaches' salaries and the work entailed in identifying job opportunities and administering the service. This arrangement too can be seen as a reciprocal relationship, this time between the public and the private sector. It is an arrangement that enables people with intellectual disability to join the workforce, thereby increasing inclusion and the number of those being gainfully employed – with all the economic and social benefits that the two factors bring with them.

Another noteworthy comment on the opening excerpt regards Noli mentioning how Ana helps her family 'not to be afraid', touching on a very important issue. Because of their ongoing support needs, persons with intellectual disability tend to continue depending on their families, especially parents, well into their adulthood (Burke et al. 2020). The primary caregivers of young people with intellectual disability can experience stress during the time the latter leave compulsory education. Parents in the study by McKenzie et al. (2017) liken it to the moment their child was diagnosed with a disability, while Park (2022) identifies family-related factors as one of the major impacts on the employability of persons with intellectual disability.

Noli's reference to her family, and to Ana's work with them, is therefore a very relevant aspect of her journey into and within employment. Her family's involvement is important on a practical level. As the main providers of support, if something goes wrong with Noli's employment they are the ones who will most likely provide her with the care that she would need. The family's direct involvement in Noli's life is also an attestation of the intertwined relationships that she has with them, as well as with her employer and her job coach. Because these relationships are supportive, Noli can set out every morning to go to work at the market, earn money and move a step closer to achieving her ambition 'to live by myself, to earn money, and to be independent'. As discussed earlier, Noli living independently by herself will not necessarily mean she is entirely alone in her household, but that she has her own place in which she is supported.

The final image from Noli's work is that of her accompanying the elderly woman, with whom we have already seen her walking in the car park. The woman uses an ankle foot orthosis and a walking stick, and Noli is carrying the woman's shopping bag in her right hand and supporting her walking with her left arm. Noli herself remarks how she likes to help elderly customers with carrying their shopping, showing herself as also being aware of other people's support needs. It is a fitting image with which to end the video. It reminds us that a person with intellectual disability, like Noli, can be both a provider and a recipient of help. It also reminds us of the added value that Noli has brought to the job carved out for her.

These reminders, in turn, highlight how employment, for anyone, is a reciprocal affair and how it can be more equitable. Employers do not just provide the capital and job opportunities. Employees do not just provide their labour. All those involved in employment are on the receiving and the giving end simultaneously. Therefore, Noli's words highlight the specificities of supported employment for persons with intellectual disability at the same time as throwing light on the reciprocity and interconnectedness of good employment relations and of human relations more widely.

The image of Noli packing oranges is a culmination of the various factors that have enabled her to join the world of work. The fact that these factors have included direct customised support, from the job coach among others, does not create any irreconcilable contradiction for Noli. This is just the way things are for her and for many other persons with intellectual disability. It might also be the way for all workers, albeit in a less clearly manifest manner.

The employment of persons with intellectual disability is likely to entail state intervention, as noted above. The intermixing of private going concerns and publicly funded support may sit at odds in a culture of hypercapitalism and neoliberalism. But Noli's openness about her support needs shines a light on the unsustainability of conceiving of workers (and human beings more generally) as being entirely self-sufficient. While the needs of Noli and other workers with intellectual disability may be different – both quantitatively and qualitatively – from the majority of other employees, there is no clear-cut boundary that can divide the workforce neatly into two: dependent workers with additional support needs and fully self-sufficient workers.

One may argue that most employees are only likely to require direct support at certain times in their working lives, whereas workers with intellectual disability, such as Noli, are much more likely to require ongoing support throughout the course of their employment and on a personal level as well. However, what Noli – and Ana and Hugo – say about her employment and the way they say it, especially the refreshing sincerity with which Noli speaks about her support needs, tells us about what can be achieved when we are attentive to individual needs, cater for those needs in a way that enables people to fulfil their potential and promote reciprocal relationships in and through employment. The sphinx's adult human being can go to work with a walking stick after all.

Note

1 Excerpt taken from Inclusion Europe (2020b), *Customised employment*. YouTube https://www.youtube.com/watch?=4hVg4K65KCA. Used with permission of Inclusion Europe.

4

MARC GUARDS THE MONEY

> At 6:30 p.m., with Marc, his students and a few Bac Pro Comptabilité final year students, we went to the supermarket down the street. Marc warned his students: 'No one buys sweets, otherwise you will just stuff yourselves!' Jérémy, Noa, Éric and Hugo are not happy. This is the first time I've heard Éric express his dissatisfaction: 'We're not children, we have no right to do anything, we can't buy what we want (*disappointed tone*)!' Éric shows me ice blocks in one of the store's freezers and says: 'He might want us to buy that! (*ironic tone*)'. Marc checks all the students' purchases. Some try to buy treats, but to no avail. They have no way of circumventing Marc's advice because he is the one who has their pocket money. (. . .) The students protest, but always discreetly. Bac Pro Comptabilité final year students buy what they want, which does not happen without arousing a certain amount of jealousy on the part of Marc's students. Jonas tells me that he prefers to keep his money for other purchases, Tom and Luc too. On the way back, I ask Marc why he is behaving like a 'mother hen' with his students. He replies that Anatole has a problem with food, so it must be 'regulated'. As for the others, he prefers to keep an eye on their purchases. He is aware of being a little harsh but, according to him, it is necessary: 'I prefer to anticipate future problems, which is why I am a little harsh sometimes. By operating like this, I have no bad surprises or not too many (*smiles*)'.
>
> Lansade (2019, p. 37, italics in the original)[1]

This excerpt is from one of the research journal entries that Lansade includes in his article analysing the experiences of a group of post-secondary students with intellectual disability who form part of the unité localisée pour l'inclusion scolaire (ULIS) inclusive education programme, which caters for

DOI: 10.4324/9781003561644-4

students with disabilities in France. The students attend the same college as those who are completing the mainstream Bac Pro Comptabilité (professional baccalaureate accounting option). The journal entry from which this passage is taken was written by Godefroy Lansade, the researcher who joined a school trip to Paris for both groups of students.

Earlier in this journal entry, we learn details about the different ways in which the two groups of students are treated that are relevant to what happens in this scene. The parents of the ULIS students give the money to Marc, the ULIS programme coordinator, who also decides who will share rooms with whom and prohibits the female and male ULIS students from visiting each other in their respective rooms. In contrast, the Bac Pro Comptabilité students keep their own money, choose who to share rooms with and are free to visit each other's rooms until bedtime.

In the excerpt, the viewpoints of some of the students with intellectual disability, Marc and the researcher are included. Through the latter's perspective, we picture the scene and consider, in turn, the perspectives of the students and their teacher, the different positions from which these perspectives are expressed and the impact that these differences have on the students.

The issues foregrounded in the excerpt can be summarised in Éric's complaint: 'We're not children!' The fact that the ULIS students are part of a group that comprises non-disabled students, who are presumably of the same age, shows how they are infantilised, as Lansade's analysis of this incident underlines.

The ULIS students' physical presence in the college does not guarantee their full inclusion, a situation which is demonstrated by the different treatment they received on this trip. Although they may be physically on the same trip and in the same supermarket with the other students, the terms on which they are situated there nullify any potential for equality and inclusion that the context could otherwise have offered. Not only that, but the situation undermines the very inclusion that the ULIS programme is supposed to achieve. The contrast between the restrictions placed on the ULIS students and the relative freedom given to the Bac Pro students is patently clear for all to witness. At the supermarket, in particular, the Bac Pro students could see how the ULIS students were not given any money or allowed to buy what they wanted like they themselves could. The manifestly different rules for both sets of students reinscribe the differential societal treatment that disabled and non-disabled persons tend to experience. What appears to be an inclusionary school trip is undermined by exclusionary practices.

There may have been valid reasons for the parents of the ULIS group to entrust the money to Marc rather than giving it directly to their children. However one of the reasons given by Marc – that Anatole's food intake needs to be controlled – does not justify controlling *everyone's* food intake. The other reason – that Marc wants to keep an eye on their spending – could be motivated by the fact that some of the students may have issues with money management and need guidance on how to spend their money, as attested by other researchers (see for example Harry et al. 2017 and Scott et al. 2013).

However, regardless of how valid these reasons are, Marc's tight hold on the purse strings is problematic. His absolute control over the money means that he does not just keep an eye on the students' spending (as he claims to be doing); he also guards it closely. It is interesting to note that the French verb *garder*, from which the English 'to guard' is derived, can mean both 'to keep' and 'to guard'. It is for the latter meaning that Marc opts, motivated by the thought that if something goes wrong, if there are any 'surprises', to use his own term, he will be the one held answerable – to the parents and to the college. The risk-averse reaction therefore seems to be for the teacher's benefit to a far greater extent than it is for the students'. In fact, for the latter the risk aversion seems to be doing more harm than good.

Whatever the motivations for the students' money to be given to Marc and to be guarded by him, the effects these actions have on the ULIS students are considerable. There is a missed opportunity for the students to acquire some useful life skills, including those related to budgeting. This is because, if these students do need support with money management, it is difficult to see how they can acquire the necessary skills to start managing for themselves when the opportunity for them to practise these skills is not taken up by their teacher when it arises. Whatever the educational aims of the trip to Paris were, prospects for incidental learning from it are bypassed and the potential for the ULIS students to develop their intra- and interpersonal skills lost.

In being appointed guardian of the money – whether by himself, by the parents, by the college or a mix of the three – Marc not only has control over the students but he also assumes full responsibility for them. The students, on the other hand, have no freedom of choice and no opportunity to exercise their rights. The situation, therefore, also raises questions about freedom and control, responsibilities and rights. If, with rights come responsibilities (Ryan 2020), then with responsibilities come rights; and, if rights are closely connected to freedom (as found in the 1948 Universal Declaration of Human Rights and subsequent human rights treaties), then maintaining responsibility for someone also means maintaining control over them and affording them fewer rights. The higher the degree of responsibility, the higher the degree of control, the less scope there is for a person to exercise their rights.

Tellingly, Éric protests that '[w]e're not children, we have no right to do anything', thus linking no longer being a child with being able to exercise one's rights. Adulthood is marked by greater control over one's life and assuming responsibility for it. Concomitantly, one has greater freedom and one can claim one's rights. After all, it is when one reaches the age of majority (at 18 years in most countries) that one acquires all the rights and responsibilities that are legally and culturally typical in one's social context. As post-secondary students, the young people who went on the trip to Paris are on the cusp of adulthood. For the ULIS students, however, adulthood – and all the rights that it confers – remains nothing but a distant and possibly unattainable prospect. The infantilisation of the ULIS students on this particular school trip does not bode well for an education that could prepare them for adulthood in the mainstream of society.

Similar situations are found in other studies. For example, Björnsdóttir et al. (2015), in research on the scope for autonomy for persons with intellectual disability in Iceland, refer to the unhappiness of Karl, one of the research participants, about the way he cannot decide how to spend his money, which means he does not always get to do what he would like to do – for example, take his girlfriend out for dinner. Fullana et al. (2019) discuss how a person with intellectual disability, this time in Spain, needs to refer decisions to support staff. This person speaks positively about the situation as decisions are backed up by staff. However, the authors rightly raise the issue of how the 'backing up' happens, and whether it is a case of support staff having the last say, especially since the person says that they and their partner 'are told yes or no'.

The ULIS students, it seems, do not even get to the stage of being told 'yes' or 'no'. The opening excerpt indicates that the 'no' came even before any of them could even ask a question. Marc has full control over managing their money as well as over their activities during the trip. Alternative options could have been used. For example, Marc could have given the ULIS students the money in chunks to avoid any of them spending it all at once. Or, in line with the practice of supported decision making (Devi 2013), he could have encouraged them to discuss with him what best to spend the money on; how to make sure that they do not eat too many sweets; and how to plan the spending so that their money lasts for the duration of the trip. He could also have used different strategies with different students, according to their support needs.

As it is, the students are trapped. Since they are not considered to have the capacity to manage their own money, or even to have a discussion about its management, they are not given the opportunity to develop this capacity. And, since they are not given this opportunity, they may never be considered capable of money management. This double bind extends itself to other aspects of their education and development, including their ability to speak up for themselves, as seen below.

If Marc were to keep, rather than guard, the ULIS students' money, he would be able to reconfigure the responsibility that he assumes for the students and their money, and find ways of sharing this responsibility with them. In research carried out in Swedish homes for persons with intellectual disability, Berlin Hallrup et al. (2019) discuss how part of the service managers' responsibility is to create support structures for the residents to participate in decision-making processes. Although control is not necessarily transferred to the residents, such structures give more scope for them to exercise their agency and develop their capacity for making more autonomous decisions, and enable them to enjoy the right to 'individual autonomy including the freedom to make one's own choices, and independence' as enshrined in Article 3(a) (General principles) of the Convention on the Rights of Persons with Disabilities (2006).

The crux of the matter is thus not so much the reliance on other adults by persons with intellectual disability, but the way that those adults choose to intervene and the type of interactions they have with the persons with intellectual disability. In the case of Jérémy, Noa, Éric and Hugo – the students who are unhappy about the injunction not to buy sweets – there is certainly no evidence that Marc, their programme coordinator, engaged in any discussion or explanation. Being told 'otherwise you will just stuff yourselves' is not much of an explanation; rather, it is an admonition and a prediction, uttered with certitude, about the mistakes the students will make if they are given the money.

It is worth noting that, in the supermarket, some of the ULIS students do not protest about their inability to buy sweets because they say they prefer to keep the money for something else anyway. However, given Marc's control of their money, it is not clear whether or not they do manage to use it according to their own preferences. Presumably, Marc will have had the final word on how they spent their money anyway.

Marc justifies being 'a little harsh sometimes' as a problem-prevention strategy; but it is problems for himself that he mentions preventing. What is missing in his reply to Lansade's querying his 'mother hen' attitude is a reflection on the negative impact that his strategy has on the students themselves.

This impact can also be seen in the way that those who protest do so 'always discreetly'. Éric and his fellow students appear helpless in the face of the absolute control exerted over them, and they know it. The complaints recorded in Lansade's journal entries, presented in the article, are articulated with him, the researcher, rather than directly with the teacher. Later in his article, Lansade also presents an exchange he had with Noa, another student who fell foul of the ban on buying sweets. Lansade asks Noa why he did not tell the teacher he was unhappy about not having access to his own pocket money. The reasons Noa gives are that he would not know how to express how he is feeling, and that the teacher would not understand and would not even listen to him.

Noa's attitude also seems to be self-defeatist. The odds of him being able to articulate his complaint well, be listened to and be understood are stacked against him to such an extent that not saying anything becomes the better option, even if (as Lansade notes) Noa speaks in an annoyed tone. The annoyance is telling since it indicates that, even if Noa does nothing about the situation, it does not mean he is not aware of the injustice of it all.

This inability to speak up points to another adverse impact of Marc's draconian treatment. Not only does Noa feel that he will not be listened to, but he is also not confident of his own ability to express and stand up for himself in an effective manner. Consequently, Marc's desire to avoid any problems for himself creates another obstacle for the ULIS students' personal and social development. It is another example of the vicious cycle of lack of opportunity leading to lack of skills and lack of skills leading to lack of opportunity.

That said, even if Marc were to take a different approach to the students' money management issue and keep the money for them rather than guard it, the distinction between the teachers and the Bac Pro students as non-disabled persons and the ULIS students as persons with intellectual disability remains. To some extent, the distinction arises from the teacher–student relationship. After all, the Bac Pro students also have rules to follow, even if these allow them much more leeway than the ones imposed on the ULIS students. This leeway is a means of preparing these students for their imminent adulthood, with all the freedoms and responsibilities that come with it, as discussed earlier. The fact that the ULIS students are not treated in the same manner not only reinforces their difference from the other students; it also highlights how they are not expected to reach the same stage of independent adulthood that their non-disabled peers are being prepared for.

Differentiation is inevitable if persons with intellectual disability are to be given the support they need because of the continued dependence created by the presence of cognitive impairment and because of their particular individual needs – for example, Anatole's need to regulate his food intake. The differentiation in itself is therefore not necessarily problematic. What is problematic is when the way in which the difference is handled hinders the development of life skills that are vital for adulthood in persons who need more support than most to develop those skills, thus reinforcing their segregation. The predicament of Éric, Noa and their ULIS course mates brings to mind the complaint about labelling made in the 1970s by Ed Murphy, one of the persons with intellectual disability whose life story is told by Bogdan and Taylor (1982). Speaking about his experience of living in an institution and moving into the community, Ed says that the word 'retarded' (as it was used then) only makes sense 'if you are going to give people help' (p. 92); otherwise, it easily risks becoming a term of abuse.

Marc's aim of anticipating future problems for himself forecloses opportunities for the students to continue with their development. The responsibility of whoever is providing support is to create structures that enable persons with intellectual disability to develop their autonomy and the skills necessary to exercise it, and to make use of opportunities to practise these skills. Otherwise, persons with intellectual disability can end up remaining passive recipients and unnecessarily dependent, even within services that should enable their personal development. To speak of them as lacking agency and autonomy in such situations may well be a reflection of those around them to a far greater extent than it is a reflection of their own capacities.

Note

1 Excerpt reproduced from Godefroy Lansade. De la difficulté à être reconnus « capables » et « compétents » : des adolescents et jeunes adultes désignés handicapés mentaux en quête d'autonomie. The difficulty of being recognized as 'capable' and 'competent': Adolescents and young adults designated as mentally disabled in search of autonomy. *Alter: European Journal of Disability Research*, 13(1), pp. 29–42. Copyright © 2019, Alter, European Society for Disability Research, published by Elsevier Masson SAS. All rights reserved. Translated version from the original French used with permission of the author.

5

EVE HAS HER PICTURE TAKEN

FIGURE 5.1 Eve has her picture taken

Source: Graham Miller

> It forced me to search my soul and think about what it is to be human and what we think is human. Down's Syndrome is not as important as I first thought, but it is tough. . . .
>
> (Lesley, Eve's mother)[1]

This quotation and double-spread photograph are taken from Graham Miller's photobook *Six Percent* (2013), which features eight families of persons with Down syndrome, most of whom were very young children at the time the photographs were taken, including Eve herself. As with the

DOI: 10.4324/9781003561644-5

two pages reproduced here, the use of text throughout the book is minimal. It provides enough details for each family's story to emerge, but it is the photographs that are left to speak for themselves.

Like all the other photographs in Miller's book, this one is in black and white, enabling a focus on the subject and on the composition without any colours to distract the eye. The foreground and sides in this photograph are blurred. A person sits on the left of the photo – to Eve's right – but the face is not included in the frame. To the right – and therefore to Eve's left – there is the blurred silhouette of another person whose arms stretch into the blurred foreground. This blurring contrasts sharply with the camera's focus on Eve and her mother Lesley. Lesley is looking intently at Eve, who is gazing into the distance; and it is her face that we can see almost fully. The text is in white at the bottom left-hand corner, superimposed on the blurred foreground, and thus as unobtrusive as possible.

The composition and presentation of the photograph invite us to direct our focus mostly on Eve herself. It is, after all, her story that we are told, albeit from the perspective of her parents. The photograph invites us to share this intimate moment between Eve and Lesley, even if they are not looking at the camera, and therefore at the viewer.

The photograph could be that of any mother and child – if it were not for Eve's eyes, which are typical of persons who have Down syndrome. And, even with those telling eyes, the photograph is still that of a mother and child or a child and mother. And yet, it is a fact that Eve and the other nine persons who feature in Miller's book together with their families do have Down syndrome, and that they and their families are affected by it. After all, if it were not for this shared characteristic, they would not have featured in the book. Another characteristic that comes across in the photo stories of all nine families is that each daughter and son with Down syndrome is very much accepted as they are as part of their respective family. Down syndrome is and is not part of the family picture at one and the same time.

Lesley refers to this ambiguous relationship with her daughter. Her words, quoted above, indicate that her search to understand what it means to be human was initiated by her having a child with Down syndrome; and yet she reflects that 'Down's Syndrome is not as important as I first thought'. Then she adds, 'but it is tough . . .'. As readers we can fill in what is left unsaid, what is marked by the ellipsis. Down syndrome is often accompanied by health issues, some of which are mentioned by some of the families whose stories feature in *Six Percent* as well as in other literature. These include a higher risk of miscarriage, mentioned by Fiona's and Ruby's parents; health problems that lead to the need for a stay in a special care unit (Bérubé 1998) or a nasogastric tube as with Ruby; the coexistence of autism and other difficulties as with Corinne; and cardiac problems (Constantine et al. 2021) and ear, nose and throat (ENT) problems (Shott 2006), among others. To these, of course, must be added the presence of cognitive impairment (Startin et al. 2016) and developmental delay (Danielsson et al. 2016), which require early intervention (Del Guidice et al. 2006) and support throughout the person's life (Roll and Bowers 2019). Children with Down syndrome thus have care and support needs that are not experienced by typically developing children (Choi and Van Riper 2020) and parents, in turn, need to be supported as well (Hsiao and Van Riper 2011).

For Eve and her family, life with Down syndrome has proved to be tough. The difficulties mentioned in her story include her stay in a special care unit because of feeding problems, and the breakdown of her parents' relationship when she was six months old.

Having a child with Down syndrome means having to cope with unforeseen difficulties. Bingham et al. (2012) note that the diagnosis of a child's disability is, for the parents, 'an initiation into a previously foreign world' (p. 372). This comment brings to mind Emily Perl Kingsley's well-known essay 'Welcome to Holland' (1987). Kingsley, whose son has Down syndrome, compares having a child with disability with planning a trip to Italy and ending up in Holland instead. Rather than focusing on what has been missed by not going to Italy, Kingsley argues, one needs to focus on not missing the beauty of Holland itself.

Shifting this focus necessitates adjustment to having a different child from the one the parents were imagining. The adjustment process is described in terms of bereavement and death by some of the parents who feature in the book, as Miller himself comments. In her analysis of narratives by parents of children born with a disability, Alison Piepmeier (2021) also notes how many of them start by describing emotions related to grief, until a turning point is reached through the affirmative aspects of the experience of having and raising a child with a disability, as the relationship with that child develops over time.

The fact that Down syndrome can be diagnosed prenatally means that prospective parents have a choice to make, and most choose to terminate the pregnancy. In statistics provided at the start of the Miller's book, we read that, after prenatal diagnosis of Down syndrome, 91 per cent of foetuses are aborted, another 3 per cent are miscarried or are stillbirths and 6 per cent are live births; hence the title of the book – *Six Percent*. It is worth noting that these statistics date from 2010, when the only test available was carried out through invasive amniocentesis. With the advent of non-invasive prenatal testing, these percentages might change (Phillips 2018, Rodríguez Díaz 2019).

Piepmeier (2021) discusses the experience of those who carry out the test and continue with the pregnancy, arguing that it can be a very difficult decision to take. The difficulties arise not only from the harmful influence of misconceptions and negative stereotypes about disability, but also from the attitude of family members and friends. Once the decision to have the baby is taken, having a positive result becomes a way of adjusting to the new reality and preparing for the additional needs of the new baby.

Reactions from other people, once the baby is born, can also be extremely hurtful. When Kenny, Eve's father, remarried he found 'a Sympathy card had been posted through the door containing a condom and the message "No more retards"' (Miller 2013, p. 108). Sympathy cards, sent when someone dies, are the polar opposite of the cards usually sent to congratulate parents on their new child. The message of the card sender is that they would rather Eve had not been born at all. Siblings too can bear the brunt of this stigma, as happened to Corinne's siblings, whose story also features in *Six Percent*. Her sister Ellis says: 'I was the girl with the sister who has Down's Syndrome' (p. 124). Life with a child with Down syndrome is tough not simply because of the additional support needs and health issues, but also because of the harmful effects of stigma and prejudice.

Adverse reactions from others towards the child with Down syndrome reinforce the message that people with Down syndrome are not automatically accorded the same status as other human beings. Perhaps these reactions, epitomised by Eve's father Kenny receiving a sympathy card for a living child, contributed to Lesley being prompted to 'search [her] soul and think about . . . what we think is human'. For Lesley, as for Kenny and all the other parents who feature in the book, having a child with Down syndrome does not subtract anything from their humanity. It is perhaps in this sense that Down syndrome is not important for Lesley, because having that extra 21st chromosome is irrelevant to Eve's inclusion in the folds of humanity.

Kenny, Eve's father, and Wilson, her grandfather, echo Lesley's words. Kenny says that her Down syndrome 'was immediately forgotten about and has been since' (p. 106), and Wilson that 'it makes no difference' (p. 105). Their words are further echoed by some of the parents who feature in the other stories.

But what is it that Down syndrome does and does not make a difference to? Clearly, as seen above, it does make a significant difference. First of all, at a pragmatic level, having a child with Down syndrome makes a difference because of the additional care and support needs. Secondly, it also makes a difference because parents tend to need a period of adjustment since, as Bryan – the father of Cameron who also features in the book – puts it: 'You've lost the child you want and got the child that you've got' (p. 62). And, thirdly, it makes a difference because of the negative attitudes that persons with Down syndrome and their families have to deal with.

Perhaps what Kenny and the other parents mean when they state that their child's Down syndrome does not make a difference, what they are referring to, is their relationship with that child – to the child being as much a part of the family as their siblings, if there are any, and to their love for that child. In fact, despite all the difficulties encountered, families of children with Down syndrome have been shown to be capable of coping and thriving (Choi and Van Riper 2020). Reflecting on their research with over 200 primary caregivers of children with Down syndrome in Australia, Povee et al. (2012) observe that the families gave an 'overriding impression of normality' (p. 971), which runs counter to widespread ideas that having a child with intellectual disability is a pervasively negative experience. These ideas have a large role to play in the decision taken by prospective parents to terminate pregnancies of foetuses with Down syndrome (Piepmeier 2021).

It seems as if, once the adjustments that need to be made are made, families of children with Down syndrome – or other types of intellectual disability – find their own sense of normality. Kittay (2019a) speaks of adjusting to a 'new normal', while Bérubé (1998) called his family account *Life As We Know It*. In the parents' narratives discussed by Piepmeier (2021), as well as her own narrative of the experience of raising Maybelle, who was born with Down syndrome, this pattern of adjustment also emerges. Adjustments do have to be made to live with a new and unexpected reality. Acceptance does not come automatically in most families, but entails a process. Preconceived plans and expectations of having a typically developing baby are disrupted as they clash with preconceived negative notions of cognitive impairment. The way that parents adjust differs as it is dependent on various factors, including the nature of the child's impairment, the type and adequacy of the support they are given and other people's attitudes towards the child.

Adjustments have been made by the nine families featured in *Six Percent*, acceptance has come to them. Implicitly or otherwise, the parents have accepted that – even if they could choose whether or not to have children – they cannot choose which children to have. As Kittay (2019b) argues in her discussion of the ethics of prenatal testing and selection, families are not exclusive clubs that get to choose who can or cannot be a member.

Additionally, for these and many other parents and families, Down syndrome (or any other condition that causes cognitive, physical or other types of impairment) is part of the picture; but it does not take anything away from the affected family member's status as a human being. It does not add anything either because it is not an add-on but an integral part of who they are. To continue with Kittay's argument, just like non-disabled offspring, these children are not burdens. However burdensome the condition may be, it is not they who are burdens.

Neil, another father who features in *Six Percent*, is quoted as saying: 'I had read somewhere somebody had said they wouldn't change their baby having Down's Syndrome for the world, and it's true because Ruby wouldn't be Ruby' (p. 150). Neil factors Ruby's Down syndrome into her identity and into the equation that accords her equal status as other children, including her twin sister Darby. It is significant that Neil's words are placed with the last photograph in the book. It is a fitting end to a book that celebrates the lives of nine persons with Down syndrome and their families.

Absent from the text accompanying the photographs in Miller's book is the voice of the children and adults with Down syndrome themselves. The focus is on how their families relate to them. The photographs, on the other hand, are mostly about them. In most, though not all, of the photographs they are not alone, but are shown in relation to family members. In most, though not all, of the photographs they are smiling. If the background is showing, it reveals surroundings we can relate to – a bedroom, a sitting room, a street, a gym, for example.

In the case of Eve's photograph shown here, we do not have the background, but she is in the embrace of her mother. She is surrounded by those who love her. As Eve gazes into the distance with eyes that indicate a pensive mood, we get a sense of security around her. At this early stage in her life, Eve is in a protective and nurturing environment which she needs as much as any other very young human being. Given that *Homo sapiens* is a highly altricial species, human babies and children continue to be highly dependent on the care of adults for a significant time. Consequently, our development as human beings is highly impacted by the environment and our interactions with those around us, and no two developmental processes are identical, not even in monozygotic twins (Deater-Deckard et al. 2001).

Nonetheless, there are enough similarities in the development process of most children for various child development theories – such as those propounded by Piaget and Vygotsky (Veraksa and Samuelsson 2022) – to provide knowledge about and insight into this process. For children with intellectual disability, the developmental trajectory is likely to be different from that which is typically observed, and their support needs are likely to continue well into adulthood. But it is still the development of a human being.

Whether or not children with intellectual disability get the opportunity to follow their own developmental trajectory and enjoy its possibilities to the full depends heavily on how others view them and whether or not they are seen as rights holders, especially as per the Convention on the Rights of Persons with Disabilities (2006). In turn, how others view children and adults with intellectual disability depends at least partly on how they are projected. When it comes to photographs of persons with intellectual disability, what is shown can tell us more about the person behind the camera than the one in front of it. In fact, the photographs of Eve and the other persons with Down syndrome who feature in Miller's book stand in sharp contrast with photographs that appeared in eugenicist books in the first half of the twentieth century. These photographs, some of which are reproduced and commented on by Bogdan (2012), completely dehumanise their subjects – who are presented against a plain background with a focus on their physical anomalies that are assumed to demonstrate their cognitive impairment.

In his own book of photographs of disabled persons, Bogdan refers to the rhetoric of these photographs. The period covered in his book ranges from the 1860s to the 1970s – that is, from when advancements in camera technology made taking photographs easier than it had ever been to when the effects of the demands of the disability rights movement began to be felt also in how disabled persons are represented in culture. Bogdan argues that one needs to take into account the broader historical and cultural backdrop to the photographs, the purpose for which they were taken and what is included or absent in each photograph.

Therefore, the photographer's view of persons with intellectual disability affects how the person being photographed is portrayed and presented. The link between the two is a metaphor for the impact that attitudes about persons with intellectual disability have on their lives. Miller's subjects, in fact, are presented with their humanity intact. They are not human despite having Down syndrome. They are human beings who happen to have Down syndrome. Whatever biological and social impacts having Down syndrome will have on their lives, their human dignity remains intact.

Surrounded by those who love her, Eve could not yet know about all the issues raised by having a child with Down syndrome, whether they are related to cognitive impairment, physical health or prejudice. But the world into which she has been thrust knows, and much depends on how that world looks at her and relates to her. Like any other human being, Eve will incorporate her relations with others and others' relations with her in her own sense of self. Asking what we see and who we see as we gaze at Eve in this photograph are therefore very important questions.

Note

1 Photograph from pages 98–99 of Graham Miller, 2013. *Six Percent – Down's Syndrome: My Photographs their Stories*. Photohonesty Publishing. Reproduced with permission of Graham Miller, and Eve and Lesley.

6

GIACOMO AND GIOVANNI GO TO THE CARNIVAL

> And then everything happened on the same day: the day of the carnival.
>
> On Sunday, 19 February, I woke up later than usual, but clear in my mind there was the promise I had made to Giovanni a few days before: to take him to the carnival floats parade. He was so excited that the only reason he didn't jump on my bed at dawn to wake me up was maybe because my parents had convinced him that I would keep my promise if he let me sleep enough.
>
> And so, after breakfast, we went down to the cellar together to rummage through what in our family we called *the big box of follies*, an enormous trunk where we throw all that sooner or later we could need to dress up, make a joke or things like that. I took a white wig, a witch's hat, a pair of tight-fitting pink trousers and a clown's nose; he a blue wig, green trousers with a dragon's tail, a red matador jacket and elf's ears; on top of all this, he wore an orange jacket, which already looked like a disguise, even if it wasn't.
>
> [. . .]
>
> Anyway, a quarter of an hour's walk, and there we were, in the square.
>
> A lot of people, practically all of Castelfranco. Every ten seconds we met a friend, a school mate, a parent one had to say hello to. And to say hello there was I, my white wig, my pink trousers and Giovanni.
>
> All together.
>
> Without embarrassment.
>
> It was one of those things that do not have an explanation; one of those things that happen and that's it.
>
> Mazzariol (2020, pp. 131–132, italics in the original)[1]

This excerpt is taken from Giacomo Mazzariol's account – which he wrote when he was 18 – of growing up with Giovanni, his younger brother who has

DOI: 10.4324/9781003561644-6

Down syndrome, and with their parents and two sisters. The event described took place when Giacomo was 15 and Giovanni ten years old. For the latter, going to the carnival with his brother was a fun occasion. For Giacomo, it was a momentous one. After spending most of his adolescence keeping the fact that he had a brother with Down syndrome a secret from anyone who did not know his family well, he was out in public with Giovanni in their hometown, Castelfranco. Giacomo was not just going out with Giovanni; he was also coming out to his community as the sibling of a child with Down syndrome. This coming out happened during carnival – a time when people can dress up and, with impunity, pretend to be someone they are not, and temporarily suspend social rules and conventions.

Giacomo and Giovanni's ill-matching clothes and funny accessories do not disguise their identity. After all, they did not wear masks and were recognisable by the various friends and acquaintances who greet them. These greetings, Giacomo tells us perhaps somewhat hyperbolically, happen every ten seconds. The hyperbole highlights the momentousness of the occasion, when he finally put behind him the years during which he was leading a double life – as Giovanni's loving brother with his family and as a boy with only two sisters to almost everyone else. His denial of Giovanni's existence, and his pretending to be something other than he was, was so complete that, two years earlier, Giacomo had found himself unable to name his favourite band during a class discussion. This incident happened two months after an unpleasant encounter with a schoolmate whom no one liked, who showed him that he knew about Giovanni's existence – an encounter that threw Giacomo off balance as his two lives threatened to clash. Sometime later, when Giacomo had to take his brother to the playground, what was uppermost in his mind was that he would be seen by his classmates. When some boys who attended his school were bullying his brother, Giacomo did not intervene. He was frozen by the fear of being found out as Giovanni's brother. It was the father of a girl at the playground who rescued Giovanni. It was an incident that racked Giacomo with a deep sense of shame and guilt.

The carnival scene signals Giacomo's complete break with this problematic past. At a time when breaking social conventions is the order of the day, Giacomo defies the conventions he had imbibed during his adolescence once and for all. He says that what happened that day at the carnival in Castelfranco 'was one of those things that do not have an explanation, one of those things that happen and that's it'. But there is scope for trying to find an explanation for what happened.

Giacomo's experience resonates with that of other siblings of children with intellectual disability, albeit in different ways. Giacomo recounts how, when his parents told him and his sisters that their baby brother would be special, he imagined a boy with superpowers. As Giovanni was growing up, Giacomo slowly began to realise that the 'specialness' of his baby brother was linked to his developmental limitations. His biggest disappointment was that Giovanni would not learn to ride a bicycle, and that he needed to adapt the way he played with him. Similarly, in research carried out in Belgium by Moyson and Roeyers (2012), Dwieke (aged 12) describes how she has to guide her brother in how to play dominos, 'so we play without winning or losing' (p. 93). But the biggest challenges for most of these families emanate not from the home but from the outside world. In *Riding the Bus with My Sister*, Rachel Simon (2002) recounts how she did not greet her sister Beth, who was sitting on the doorstep when Rachel was stepping down from the school bus. That was a moment when, like Giacomo's, Rachel's inner and outer persona threatened to clash.

There are reasons for siblings like Giacomo and Rachel to act in this way. One of Giacomo's painful experiences was when he overheard three boys making fun of people with Down syndrome. Manni Coe, whose brother Reuben also has Down syndrome, describes how people who did not know his family well stared at them (Coe and Coe 2022). Likewise, Marie, another participant in Moyson and Roeyers' (2012) research, mentions that what creates most discomfort for her is when the family goes out 'for a walk with her, then people really are staring at her and at us! Perhaps this isn't meant badly, but still . . .' (p. 97). At 12 years old, Marie shows a maturity that seems to escape many adults. These experiences highlight the clash between, on the one hand, a family home in which parents and disabled and non-disabled siblings live well together and whose bonds withstand problems that crop up; and, on the other, scholastic and various community settings where having a disability (especially an intellectual disability) devalues a person and the life of a much-loved sibling.

One response to this clash is that of Giacomo. Since he attended a different secondary school to his primary school classmates, he could start an alternative life to the one he had at home, one in which his youngest sibling did not exist. Like the adolescents in Corsano et al.'s (2017) Italian research and some of the children in a UK study by Pavlopolou et al. (2022), Giacomo did not often invite friends home, and only did so when he knew his brother would not be there.

Another occasion on which Giacomo's two lives nearly crashed into each other was when he invited his bandmates to play in their garage while Giovanni was supposed to be out with their mother. But his mother changed her plans and asked Giacomo to take care of his younger brother while she went out on her own. Giacomo was as concerned about his brother's welfare as he was about his status with his friends. In order not to upset Giovanni, he did not forbid him outright from leaving his bedroom or specify that he did not want him to be seen by his friends. Instead, he enticed him to stay in the bedroom by lending him his iPod and nice headphones to listen to music while looking at his favourite dinosaur books. Giacomo's reactions are contradictory – loving his brother while keeping his existence secret, silently begging his forgiveness. Similar findings of ambiguous attitudes are found in Corsano et al.'s (2017) research with siblings of children on the autism spectrum, most of whom report that they 'expressed both annoyance and empathy toward their brother' (p. 156), and in the Netherlands-based study by Luijkx et al. (2016) with siblings of children with profound intellectual and multiple disabilities, tellingly titled 'I love my sister, but sometimes I don't'.

The Convention on the Rights of Persons with Disabilities (2006) upholds the right of Giovanni and all other siblings with intellectual disability to be accepted both in their own home and in the community. Article 23 (Respect for home and the family) asserts the right of children with disabilities to be raised in their own family and not be taken away from it on the basis of their disabilities. Article 19 (Living independently and being included in the community) asserts the right of persons with disabilities to be active members of their own communities, outside their homes. What Giacomo's account, and that of other siblings of children and adults with intellectual disability, shows us is that these two rights are connected. Families of children with disabilities often need support from outside the home to be able to cater to their needs, as Article 23 also asserts. They also need to be able to go out into their communities and be accepted, just like any other family would be. Exclusion from the community can happen through a lack of adequate support services, lack of accessibility, adverse attitudes or a combination of all three. The sibling accounts cited above show that this exclusion does not just hurt the chances of a person with disability from participating in the community. They also hurt them and their family at a very personal level. What Giacomo did on Sunday, 19 February was push back against the hurtful attitudes – his and those of the community – to make his relationship with his brother whole again.

The title of the chapter from which the opening excerpt is taken – 'Spak, Frush, Snap' – betokens a sudden change in Giacomo. But the scene described in the excerpt is also a crucial turning point in a process which had started two years earlier as Giacomo started to learn to accept his brother as he was not only within the safe boundaries of his family, but also in the wider world. In the end, it took that 15-minute walk for Giacomo to meld together his private and public personae in the town square, an open area where he was likely to be seen by most people. On the day when '[a] lot of people, practically all of Castelfranco', were out, Giacomo went out with the brother whose existence he had hidden from the very people he was now greeting '[w]ithout embarrassment'. At the time of year when pretence and disguise are the order of the day, he showed in public this hitherto concealed aspect of his life, of his identity. Just like Giovanni's orange jacket, Giacomo's outfit 'looked like a disguise, even if it wasn't'. On the day when going out with a mask to cover one's real identity is the norm, Giacomo shed the mask he had been wearing for years.

Giacomo's change was radical. From hiding Giovanni's existence from anyone who did not know his family closely, he went on to proclaim it to the world, starting from *The Simple Interview* on YouTube (Jack N John 2015). Since then, he has also given many interviews on Italian television, and the prize-winning *Mio Fratello Rincorre i Dinosauri* has been translated into many languages, is used as a school textbook and has also been made into a film.

Giovanni did have a powerful effect on his older brother's life, but not in the way that the latter had imagined when he and his sisters were told that their new baby brother was special. As he himself says in a short video (Premio Sciacca 2016), he chose to enter his brother's world and accept it as it is, even when it goes against conventional behaviour. It is a world in which Giovanni stops to pick daisies while playing football, and in which, as long as he used the word 'dinosaurs' in the title, Giacomo could write about their life. It is also a world in which the 13-year-old Giovanni sees fit to leap on stage during a summer camp recital of *The Lion King* to prevent the actor playing Simba from winning a fight with the one playing Scar because his sympathy was with the latter. Most importantly, as Giacomo says in the Premio Sciacca video, it is a world in which he chose to love the person next to him unconditionally and even find joy in sharing his life with him, like Leo Kittay did in being Sesha's brother (Kittay and Kittay 2000).

Giacomo's transformation is epitomised by what he does on the day of the carnival. The irony of the situation highlights the dramatic nature of Giacomo's transformation. From being a boy who was keen to conform to what he perceived as being socially acceptable, he defies carnival conventions by publicly embracing his authentic self in front of the whole town. Thus, it is the very public manner of Giacomo's 'coming out' that constitutes the abrupt change signalled in his chapter's title and the excerpt quoted in this chapter.

Furthermore, by announcing himself to be Giovanni's brother, Giacomo shows that he has learnt to accept his brother as he is – as a person who is oblivious of conventional expectations, whether it is carnival or not. And, while the convention-defying rules of carnival are temporary, Giacomo's radical change is life-long. A parallel process can be seen in Rachel Simon's (2002) account of how joining her sister Beth's bus rides over the course of a year enabled her to appreciate life from Beth's perspective and to change the way she looked at her own life, shedding normative expectations and re-evaluating what was important in her life.

Where is Giovanni in all this? And where are Beth, Reuben, Sesha and all the persons with intellectual disability who have a lasting effect on their siblings' lives? The value of their lives obviously does not lie only in what they can teach others. But the transformative nature of relationships with them highlights at least two very important points.

First of all, these siblings' experiences show how the childhood experiences of persons with intellectual disability can be different to those of non-disabled children. Even if they grow up in the same family, even if their childhoods overlap with those of their siblings, many persons with intellectual disability do not share in all the activities of their brothers and sisters and of other children their age. Some of the differences relate to their impairment-related needs. Others arise from the world outside the family home which the siblings tend to find ways to navigate for themselves. Persons with intellectual disability, on their part, tend to inhabit two worlds. With those who are disposed to get to know them well, as fellow human beings, they are accepted for who they are and they flourish. With those who are unwilling to get to know them as persons in their own right and who only react to the outward manifestations of cognitive impairment through preconceived negative notions, their lives are devalued and they suffer. Sibling accounts, therefore, also highlight just how precarious the lives of persons with intellectual disability can be, how dependent their welfare is on interactions with persons who value their lives and their human dignity. Manni Coe's account of the neglect suffered by his brother Reuben in various service settings attests to that (Coe and Coe 2022). These siblings might very well ask the same question that the adolescent Giacomo asks: 'How was I going to manage to live with my brother's fragility?' (Mazzariol 2020, p. 67).

Possible answers to Giacomo's question connect with the second important point regarding the lives of Giovanni and other persons with intellectual disability. Giacomo's account, as well as that of other siblings and family members of persons with intellectual disability, shows that the answer to that question is not to treat persons with intellectual disability as passively waiting to be protected from a hostile world. The answer is to accept them as they are and to show the world that they are as capable of forming reciprocal and dynamic relationships as much as anyone else, and regardless of how severe their cognitive impairment might be. It is not enough to be loving and accepting towards persons with intellectual disability in the privacy of the home. They also need to be accepted in their immediate community and in wider society.

In learning to accept Giovanni for who he is, both privately and publicly, Giacomo lived a watershed moment, embodied in accompanying his brother to the carnival at Castelfranco, saying hello to the world without a mask, and with his white wig, his pink trousers and Giovanni. The wig and trousers were soon put away again in 'the big box of follies'. The mask is never put on again. What remains is the wisdom Giacomo gained from embracing Giovanni's idiosyncratic take on the world, regardless of whether it is in line with social conventions or flies in their face.

Note

1 Excerpt taken from pages 131–132 of Giacomo Mazzariol, 2020. *Mio Fratello Rincorre i Dinosauri* [*My Brother Chases Dinosaurs*]. © 2016 and 2018 Giulio Einaudi editore s.p.a., Turin. Own translation from the original Italian.

7

LAUREN FACES THE CAMERAS

> **Lauren** (guest): I really love being in front of camera. I love having people to watch me and seeing me play the part of the other person. It was so much fun to be someone else. But a little bit while I love comedy roles like Glee and drunk history but don't worry I wasn't really actually drunk but I also loved doing dramas like Chicago med and Guest room. I love working with other actors and actresses and the great awesome crew and being on set. It is my dream come true wow.
>
> Episode 176 of *DNA Today: A Genetics Podcast* (2022)[1]

This excerpt is from a podcast interview with Lauren Potter, the actor who is well known for her role as Becky in the US television series *Glee*. Her career also includes roles in episodes of various other series, including *Chicago Med* and *Veep*, as well as featuring as herself in an episode of the reality show *Born This Way*. Additionally, she has appeared in some films, and produced and stars in the short film *The Guest Room* (Tate 2015). Lauren also features in many interviews and speeches, available online, in which she uses her fame to campaign for the rights of persons with intellectual disability. Lauren has Down syndrome.

In the extract above, Lauren talks about playing 'the part of the other person'. This is, after all, what actors do. The roles that she has played are varied, which shows her versatility as an actor. While there is no doubt that the characters that Lauren has portrayed are fictional personas, the fact that – like her characters – she has Down syndrome plays a significant part in the roles that she interprets. The distinctive features of Down syndrome are

DOI: 10.4324/9781003561644-7

an inherent part of Lauren's embodied presence on screen, so much so that, inevitably, her characters also have Down syndrome.

In this excerpt, it is being an actor, and presenting herself to viewers in the role of other persons, that Lauren says she loves. Given her achievements, she is well within her rights to enjoy her success as an actor. But she is of course also not just any actor, but an actor with Down syndrome. In disability studies, especially within that portion of it that Bolt (2018) calls 'cultural disability studies', the representation of disabled people in film and television, whether by disabled persons themselves or by non-disabled persons, receives a lot of attention. Discussions include critiques of the representation of persons with intellectual disability such as the ones by Benjamin Fraser in *Cognitive Disability Aesthetics* (2018), where he argues that '[t]he material experience of disability in film has the potential to correct the pervasive and historical effects of the normative stigmatization of cognitive disabilities' (p. 66). Since film is an audiovisual medium, the embodiment of actors with disability is an inevitable part of their role. This applies to actors with intellectual disability as well, including Sarah Gordy, Tommy Jessop and Madison Tevlin, who, like Lauren Potter, have Down syndrome. When they appear in film or on stage, they produce a visual – and highly visible – representation of intellectual disability.

Their acting work has various dimensions. They are actors with Down syndrome who represent characters with Down syndrome, through whom viewers learn more about the day-to-day lives of persons with Down syndrome and other forms of intellectual disability and the disabling barriers they tend to encounter. Their presence on screen or on stage refutes widespread ideas about the supposed incompetence of persons with intellectual disability. For example, Jessop's role in *Innocence* (Reid 2019) turns expectations of persons with intellectual disability as helpless victims of crime on their head. Typically, the storylines they feature in are a part of what the Polish theatre company Teatr 21 – which comprises actors with Down syndrome and autism – calls 'universal topics . . . dreams being confronted with reality, about aspirations, about work, or rather unemployment, about love, desire, friendship, family' (cited by Siedlecka-Dorosz 2020, pp. 201–202). Each of these four actors can say, like Gordy (2020), 'I'm a professional actor – I'm not "professionally Down's syndrome"' (p. 59).

Concomitantly, in a move that reflects the role of disability politics in film and the role of film in disability politics, all four actors actively campaign on issues that are important for persons with intellectual disability. Therefore, while in the quotation from the podcast Lauren speaks about having fun playing someone else and loving the fact that people see her playing 'the part of the other person', the experiences of the other persons whose parts she plays have a close correlation with those of persons who, like her, have an intellectual disability.

Consequently, even while speaking about herself as an actor (full stop), Lauren also presents herself as an actor with Down syndrome, speaks about herself as a person with Down syndrome and raises issues of concern for people with Down syndrome and other types of intellectual disability. Interestingly, in various interviews and speeches by Lauren which are available online, she does not speak much about her acting experience. In the podcast interview, Kira, the host, asks Lauren mostly about her experiences as a person with Down syndrome and her campaigning work. In fact, the excerpt in this chapter is practically the only comment about herself where Lauren specifically discusses her work as an actor.

As a campaigner, she uses her acting experience and her fame as an actor really well as a platform for activism. In an interview on the Seattle-based *Take Five* television chat show, Lauren speaks about being in that city to campaign against 'the R word' and wanting to stop bullying of persons with intellectual disability. She made a speech at a conference of Best Buddies International (2012), an organisation that works with people with individual and developmental disabilities. Lauren is also a member of the Board of Directors of Best Buddies and was appointed Goodwill Ambassador for Special Olympics (2015). Additionally she was given a Media Access Award in 2012, among other awards, and was appointed by President Obama to the President's Committee for People with Intellectual Disabilities. Her campaigning also includes starring in the video of 'Be the One', a song about inclusion (It Starts With a Voice 2013), and an advert for people to stop using the 'R' word in which she features alongside *Glee*'s Jane Lynch (Anchor Films 2015).

In her podcast interview, Lauren tells the host Kira about how she was well suited to act as '[t]his sassy, spunky, little Becky'. Both Lauren and Kira take 'sassy' and 'spunky' to apply to Lauren as much as to her character Becky. The function of the adjective 'little' in this description of Becky is used 'as an (ironic) intensifier' as the *Oxford English Dictionary* defines this particular usage of the word (see definition 10). It highlights rather than diminishes Becky and Lauren's sass and spunk.

Despite any characteristics that Lauren might share with Becky, there remains a clear-cut distinction between Lauren and the characters that she portrays. Just like any other actor, a line can easily be drawn between her life in the real world and the fictional lives she portrays on screen, between the sober Lauren and her drunken character for example. There is nonetheless a close link between Lauren's acting work and the campaigning work that she does on behalf of people with Down syndrome and other intellectual disabilities, a link that is much closer than that which other well-known actors may have with causes they support or campaign for.

In fact, Lauren's work is self-referential. Her fictional work portrays real-life experiences and difficulties of people with intellectual disability.

Campaigning for the latter is enhanced by the fictional work. Lauren's appearance and presence is marked by the physical features that clearly manifest her Down syndrome, whether she is facing the camera while pretending to be someone else or speaking as Lauren. The two aspects of her work complement each other and are as distinguishable from each other as they are interconnected.

A brief analysis of Tate's *The Guest Room* can illustrate this point. In this 12-minute film, Lauren, who is also one of the executive producers, plays Amber. In the film's opening scene, Amber is having sex with her boyfriend Michael. A minute into the film, the main plotline is revealed – the couple have forgotten to use a condom, with the consequence being that she becomes pregnant.

The film is mostly about sexuality and parenting and the difficulties that persons with intellectual disability encounter in these areas of human experience. From the beginning, it sets out to challenge stereotypes and misconceptions. Starting a narrative about persons with intellectual disability with an intimate scene in the bedroom is bound to confound assumptions of their being innocent and asexual. In this regard, it is an excellent tool to raise discussions about sexuality and related issues and the rights enshrined in Article 23 (Respect for the home and the family) of the Convention on the Rights of Persons with Disabilities (2006). It features, for example, in an article in the online magazine *Parenting Special Needs* (2016).

The Guest Room also goes beyond the sex and its resulting pregnancy. Amber is staying overnight with Michael and his parents in their home, on the eve of Michael's birthday party. Amber seems to be just like any other young woman until the moment Michael's mother, over breakfast, reminds her that she needs to tell her sister if she wants to stay over for a second night, after the party. Amber is not happy about this remark. It is a reminder that she is not like other adults after all. Another reminder comes soon afterwards when Amber is in the hairdresser's salon, where she works as an assistant, and the moment she picks up a pair of scissors is addressed as 'sweetheart' by the hairdresser, who then tells her 'to be careful please'. Amber's look of irritation is juxtaposed by the customer praising the hairdresser because he is 'very good with her'. The only person who seems to treat Amber as an equal is her sister. There's no condescension in her voice, nothing to suggest that she is consciously speaking to someone with Down syndrome.

The contrast in attitudes comes to the fore with the way the issue of Amber and Michael having a baby is spoken about. Michael's parents first have a talk with him and then with Amber. It is the mother who does most of the talking, with a mixture of being supportive and pointing out that they need to be extra careful because their 'children have a 50% chance of . . .', with the words 'having Down syndrome' remaining unspoken. Perhaps she realises that saying those words would hurt the young couple, as she finds herself caught between respecting them as young adults while also speaking about preventing having babies like them. It is Amber's sister, who herself has a very young baby, who does not see the Down syndrome issue as problematic. Her reaction is: 'So? So what? You turned out all right.' The camera then focuses on the baby, as if to reinforce the point that all babies are equal after all.

Amber's sister's words are the last ones spoken in this short film and they are echoed in the way that, in the podcast, Lauren speaks of having Down syndrome as being 'just different' – an argument which, in turn, echoes Elizabeth Barnes' argument about disability being a value neutral difference in *The Minority Body* (2016). Lauren speaks of her having 'worked harder and longer to do what most people do quickly'. But she does not consider this a difference that makes her inferior.

It is very difficult to get out of the tension between speaking of persons with cognitive impairment as different to the majority of the population that does not have cognitive impairment, and as their being just as human as that majority. This tension can also be seen in the portrayal of the adults with Down syndrome who are the protagonists of Maite Alberdi's 2016 documentary *The Grown-Ups*. As Fraser (2021) observes, in this film the camera is always on these adults, and not on their relatives or the staff who work with them. They are the ones whose perspectives we are invited to consider; it is their problems – especially that of being treated like children – that we are bidden to ponder on. Fraser (2021) writes: 'Alberdi arrives at the discourse of universal human rights for people with disabilities . . . by confronting inequities and marginalization in the lives of specific people with Down syndrome head-on' (p. 237).

In order to confront these issues, Alberdi, Lauren Potter and anyone else who campaigns for equal recognition of the rights and dignity of persons with intellectual disability will inevitably mark the latter out as different from other people even as their aim is affirming the humanity they share with everyone else and the rights that are theirs by virtue of their humanity.

Lauren's acting work is valid qua acting, especially because she is so accomplished. One only has to contrast her 'sassy and spunky' Becky with her more subdued Amber to appreciate her talent. The recognition of this talent places her in an excellent position as a campaigner as she uses her fame as an actor to carry out work such as that outlined above.

Lauren is a person like any other and a person with Down syndrome at the same time. She is also an actor like any other and an actor with Down syndrome at the same time. Judging from the way she speaks in interviews and the pride she has in her acting achievements, she also holds all these distinctions to be true of her at the same time.

It cannot really be otherwise, since when we see Lauren – whether as Lauren or as one of the characters she interprets – we also see a person with Down syndrome. Therefore, in the same way that we speak of the physically disabled body, we can speak of the intellectually disabled body. It is true that the needs of persons with intellectual disability are markedly different from those of persons with other types of disability since the former need support with cognitive processes and not only with physical activities. But, as Fraser (2018) argues, the distinctions between physical and cognitive impairment may not be as clear-cut as they are often made out to be.

Cognitive impairment does not only have an impact on the development of the brain in terms of intelligence and socially adaptive behaviour – the two main criteria for establishing the presence of cognitive impairment in a person (AAIDD 2021). It also impacts the body, with certain genetic mutations (such as the extra 21st chromosome in Down syndrome or the mutation in the FMR1 gene that causes Fragile X syndrome) leading to specific physical patterns that are recognisable even in the face of the person who has that syndrome. There are usually other physical markers on the body too, and a susceptibility to certain medical conditions as well as a tendency for problems with fine or gross motor coordination, and a particular way of speaking. Consequently, even if the main impact of cognitive impairment is in the brain it also has outward physical, and therefore visible, manifestations.

When compared to the 'normate', to use Garland-Thomson's (1997) term, these manifestations make for differences that are considered negative and place the person in an inferior position in relation to the majority of other persons. In campaigning for people not to use the 'R' word, for people with intellectual disability not to be bullied and for other issues affecting them negatively, Lauren shows that she is aware of how most people tend to look at someone who presents themselves with the markings associated with Down syndrome.

Through this campaigning, a difference emerges between the way Lauren sees herself and the way she knows others see her. This aspect of her work is based on directly highlighting this difference. By hooking on to her renown as an actor, especially as *Glee*'s Becky, in her various speeches and interviews Lauren seems to be saying: Living with Down syndrome is not at all what you think it is. Look at me, a successful actor with Down syndrome, as an example.

Her acting work, then, also highlights this difference, more indirectly. When Becky makes it on to the cheerleading team in *Glee*, it feels like a vindication for Lauren, who had not been chosen as a cheerleader at her school, as she says in the podcast interview. It is also a message to the world that a person with Down syndrome can take part in mainstream activities. When Amber finds herself dealing with her sexuality and her approaching motherhood in a world full of condescension even by the most well-meaning of people, we are invited to take an intimate, albeit brief, look at how adults with intellectual disability negotiate their place in the world.

Lauren Potter has come a long way from the day when she was not chosen for the cheerleading team at her school. She has achieved her childhood dream of becoming an actor, and uses her fame to campaign for other people with intellectual disability not to have to go through the negative experiences that she and others have had to live through. Taking a close look at her work enables us to see how, whether she is playing the part of another person or publicly speaking as Lauren, the embodiment of Down syndrome is always present and even prominent. Taking on board what she says might, just might, help us create a world in which Down syndrome does become a neutral difference.

Note

1 Excerpt taken from Episode 176 of *DNA Today: A Genetics Podcast*, 18 March 2022, hosted and produced by Kira Dineen, MS, LCGC, CG(ASCP)CM. http://dnapodcast.com/episodes/2022/3/18/176-glees-lauren-potter-on-down-syndrome-awareness. Used with permission of DNA Today.

8

PARTICIPANT 13 PUTS A SERVICE-USER IN THEIR OWN SHOES

> P13: Often you need to stand back and think, 'what would I like to do? Would I really want to do that again when I did it the same time last week, the same time the week before?' 'Cause that's what it's all about you know, asking them kind of questions, thinking about what might be best, if they're ever going to live a life like ours.
>
> Dunn et al. (2010, p. 151)[1]

The research by Dunn, Clare and Holland (2010), from which this excerpt is taken, was carried out in England with support staff working in three homes for adults with severe intellectual disability who also have additional physical, sensory or communication impairments. The analysis and discussion of the data from the researchers' interviews highlight how these support workers strive to create lives for the residents that are on a par with their own lives. Given the severity and complexity of the impairments of the service-users, navigating decision-making on a day-to-day basis is far from straightforward.

Dunn et al. situate their research in the context of a liberal society, where individuals can decide for themselves about what activities to engage in. This research focuses on leisure activities, an aspect of life which for most people is particularly amenable to the exercise of personal choices, away from the strictures of employment, full-time education and family responsibilities. The quotation above from Participant 13 is representative of most of the responses from the other support workers, as reported by the researchers. For example, P5 describes how they take residents to a disco for persons with intellectual disability once a month. While this support worker acknowledges that this is not like the nightclub that they themselves go to once a week, the arrangement is 'better than nothing' (p. 151).

DOI: 10.4324/9781003561644-8

Interestingly, the support workers do not seek to put themselves in the shoes of the service-user, but put the service-user in their own shoes. They use their own lives as a benchmark against which to compare the lives of the persons they work with. They come across as attentive to the fact that, what for them is their place of work, is home for these persons, and they would like the latter's life at home and their leisure time to be similar to theirs. The challenge faced by these support workers is to understand what choices the service-users would make if they could articulate their wishes clearly.

This challenge is also addressed by the Committee on the Rights of Persons with Disabilities (2014) in General comment No. 1 on Article 12 (Equal recognition before the law) of the Convention on the Rights of Persons with Disabilities (2006) (CRPD), 'Equal recognition before the law'. The Committee distinguish between legal capacity, which is asserted as a fundamental right belonging to all human beings, and mental capacity, which varies from one person to another and from one situation to another. The Committee argue very strongly that the response to difficulties in decision-making abilities due to a lack of mental capacity should be supported and not substitute decision-making. The former approach ensures that disabled individuals retain the ability to exercise their rights, will and preferences. In the General Comment (para. 21), the Committee also states that

> Where, after significant efforts have been made, it is not practicable to determine the will and preferences of an individual, the 'best interpretation of will and preferences' must replace the 'best interests' determinations . . . The 'will and preferences' paradigm must replace the 'best interests' paradigm to ensure that persons with disabilities enjoy the right to legal capacity on an equal basis with others.

However, rather than basing decisions on the best interpretation of the will and preferences of the service-users – on questions such as 'What would this service-user prefer to do given what we know about their likes and dislikes, their will and preferences?' – the support workers in this research ask 'What would this service-user prefer to do if they were me?', thus operating within what can be considered to be a substitute decision-making regime. By 'thinking about what might be best', as P13 puts it in the opening excerpt, the support workers also take into account what they consider to be the best interests of the disabled people they work with. But it is a very particular form of substitute decision-making and best interests approach that is being used.

The primary basis of the support workers' approach seems to be very much in line with the Golden Rule, treating the service-users as they would themselves like to be treated. This approach is reflected in P13's two questions in the quotation above. In the rest of the data presented by Dunn et al. (2010), the support workers come across as well intentioned. For instance, P5 also explains how they do not like 'to plonk them in front of the TV and go and get on with something else' (p. 152), but seek other, more stimulating activities for the residents, such as spending some time in the garden.

Furthermore, the care and support that the support workers provide to their service-users includes deliberate efforts to enable them to live a life like theirs, and thus to enjoy life on a similar basis to them. It can therefore be presumed that these support staff are working on the assumption that they are themselves living a good life, in the broadest sense of the term. They are also contributing to the enjoyment by the service-users of their right to community-based leisure activities, as per Article 30 of the CRPD (Participation in cultural life, recreation, leisure and sport).

Questions remain as to whether the residents in the three homes in Dunn et al.'s study enjoy the activities they are involved in by their support workers, and as to what ways can be used to understand whether or not they enjoy these activities. The article does not go into whether and how the support workers check if the activities in which they decide to engage the service-users are actually enjoyed by the latter. However, one could imagine how they can find out. For example, if a service-user becomes agitated every time they go to the disco or stay out in the garden, it would be easy for the support workers to identify the trigger for the agitation and avoid these activities for that particular resident.

Understanding the non-verbal communication of persons with severe intellectual and additional disabilities can, however, also be a somewhat difficult enterprise. As Griffiths and Smith (2016) point out, '[m]ost of their communications are non-verbal, often idiosyncratic and ambiguous' (p. 124). These authors stress the importance of attuning to the ways in which the person communicates, an endeavour that takes time and deliberate intention on the side of the interlocutor to reach a clear understanding of the disabled person's communication patterns. The importance of being attentive to the non-verbal communication methods of such persons is also highlighted in other research, including that by Forster and Iacono (2008), Hostyn et al. (2011) and Martin et al. (2022), among others. Furthermore, Brady et al. (2016) discuss the right to communication of persons with severe disabilities and present guidelines that call for a move away from deficit-based approaches to ones that take into account the person's adaptive abilities, their background and environmental factors.

The right of access to communication is also asserted in CRPD Article 9 (Accessibility) and Article 21 (Freedom of expression and opinion, and access to information). The latter also refers to the use of augmentative and alternative communication (AAC) as a right. According to the American

Speech-Language-Hearing Association (2023), AAC encompasses options that involve the use of technology as well as those that do not need any technology, including the non-verbal communication discussed above.

In fact, those working and living with persons with severe intellectual and multiple disabilities, including communication difficulties, can make use of assistive communication devices as part of an AAC strategy to find out more about each person's will and preferences. However, these devices on their own are not enough. As Nijs and Maes (2021) argue in their European survey, persons who need AAC devices also need assistance in using those devices since, by the very nature of their impairments, they cannot use them on their own. These authors also show the importance of using such devices as a component of the communication strategy that takes all relevant factors into account. These factors include: choosing the right device for each person; getting to know that person well; understanding how that person uses their particular device; and having positive attitudes towards the use of these devices. In their US-based study on the use of AAC with young children with complex communication needs, Ogletree et al. (2018) also refer to the need to understand how each person uses their device since they are not homogeneous, and 'commonly held assumptions about AAC symbol transparency and display are not supported by data and can limit the effectiveness of AAC users' (p. 114). The authors conclude that 'AAC providers must carefully and respectfully introduce themselves into the lives of young children and their families to create meaningful, contextually relevant, and socially valid AAC systems' (p. 120). This conclusion also applies to adults with complex communication needs. In fact, using family members as proxy informants is another important strategy in efforts to identify the will and preferences of persons with severe intellectual and multiple disabilities (Jansen et al. 2017, Kruithof et al. 2020, 2021).

There are therefore ways to elicit some answers from persons with severe to profound intellectual and additional impairments to the questions posed by P13 regarding what each service-user would like to do, if they would like to do the same thing as in previous weeks and what is best for them. These methods include taking careful note of non-verbal communication, using AAC and consulting with those who know the person well. The information obtained may not lead to conclusive answers, but it can help ensure that the best interpretation of the person's will and preferences is being used as a basis for decision-making.

The use of AAC entails a deeply interpersonal communication process. It does not only involve a reciprocal one-to-one interaction between two persons, who may or may not have a disability. As can be seen from the discussion above, the effective use of AAC requires the input of those who have gained in-depth knowledge of the person with severe intellectual and multiple disabilities, including family members and support workers. Additionally, it is these latter persons who are likely to do most of the work. In such cases, where the severity and complexity of the impairments are correlated – as they often are – with severe communication difficulties, the onus is not on the person with disability to make themselves understood; it is on those around them to take the time and make the effort to understand them as much as possible.

Furthermore, the onus is on family members, support workers and others to provide the person with severe communication difficulties with opportunities to make choices and express preferences. There is therefore another important question that needs to be addressed. This regards how to ensure that the will and preferences that the service-users are expressing are based on informed choices. For example, they cannot express an opinion on whether or not they find discos enjoyable unless they have been at least once; and they cannot signal a preference for going out in the garden or watching television on any given evening unless they have engaged in both activities. Because of their impairments, the basis on which they can make choices and express preferences, however, will not likely be built by them. It would not be realistic to expect them to actively seek to explore options for the type of activities that they can enjoy completely on their own.

Consequently, the agency of others – such as family members and staff working in service-providing organisations – needs to be engaged not only to elicit communication from persons with severe intellectual and multiple disabilities, but also to create the framework on which this communication can be based. In the case of leisure activities, this framework could be a list of activities identified by those who play a significant part in the lives of these disabled persons on the basis of what Hollomotz (2014) calls 'a menu of choices' which is set by others and restricts the options available. Within this context, asking the questions posed by P13 above seems to be a starting point.

The high level of dependence on others experienced by persons with severe intellectual and multiple disabilities means that their lives are very intricately entwined with the lives of those who provide them with support. As Kamstra et al. (2015) note, persons with these types of disabilities have difficulties developing informal support networks. Their formal relationships with family members and workers who are paid to provide them with various types of services thus take on increased importance. It is these relationships that very often provide these disabled persons with opportunities to interact with others in informal ways. The decisions taken by the support workers in Dunn et al.'s (2010) research can help create environments that provide opportunities for enjoyment and for more informal interactions between persons with severe intellectual and multiple disabilities and those whose duty it is to provide them with care and support in a formal manner. These opportunities can, in turn, create contexts in which these disabled persons can be provided with options to make informed choices from, among others, the communication strategies discussed earlier.

The high level of dependency needs experienced by persons with severe intellectual and multiple disabilities creates very close ties with those supporting them in their day-to-day lives. In a video by the Scottish organisation Promoting a more inclusive society titled *Profound Inclusion* (PAMIS 2017), various professionals and family members attest to these very close links that develop with the disabled persons they live or work with. For example, Joanna Fraser, a speech and language therapist, describes them as people who have 'great intensity'. Pat Graham, a parent, draws on the synonymous relationship between 'profound' and 'deep' that are used to refer to the deep-seated ties that must be forged to enable access to the communication of disabled persons with this profile and to interact with them. Graham also explains how 'carers are more than just carers' as they also take on the role of advocates, entertainers and educators, among others. Additionally, Claire Thould, Kaela's mother in the video, highlights how her daughter 'inspires me to be the best that I can be'. Thus, persons with severe intellectual and multiple disabilities also have a profound effect on their families and those who work with them. The video ends with the various contributors stating 'I am profound', one after the other. Although each speaker utters this statement separately, the message that comes across is that everyone is profoundly connected with others.

In fact, there may be more going on in the opening quotation from P13 than just an example of substitute decision-making based on a best-interest approach. The support workers interviewed by Dunn et al. base their decisions regarding what is best for the disabled persons they work with on the norms of the liberal society they live in, and opt for leisure activities that are typical in their own society. Thus, while these decisions are mostly based on what the support workers would have chosen for themselves, their personal choices are also influenced by pre-established structures and ideas. The difference between the decision-making processes of persons with severe intellectual and multiple disabilities and persons who can articulate choices and preferences more easily may be more a question of degree rather than quality. That is to say, the intensive needs experienced by the former and their high level of dependence on others do not make them a different kind of person. Rather, these needs are witness to the intertwined ties that we all have.

Laura Davy (2015) discusses the idea of relational autonomy, exposing the inadequacy of notions of autonomy that cast human beings as self-sufficient individuals who take decisions on a purely rational basis and entirely on their own. Instead, she calls for autonomy to 'be understood as a relational dynamic – an ongoing negotiation of the self within interdependent relationships that requires these relationships to be organized' (p. 146). Significantly, Davy extends this relational understanding of autonomy to all human beings.

The high-intensity support needs of persons with severe intellectual and multiple disabilities, the deeply intertwined ties that family, support workers and other professionals with them form with them, and the multi-faceted ways in which they communicate are thus traits that make these persons profoundly human. The opening extract starts and ends with support worker P13 putting in their own shoes the disabled residents of the home she works in by asking 'What would I like to do?' and deliberately seeking to enable them to 'live a life like ours'. Given the difficulties that arise from trying to put oneself in the shoes of a person with severe intellectual and multiple disabilities, of reaching an adequate understanding of what their own embodied experience is like, reversing the process by putting them in one's own shoes may not be a bad place to start at all. Doing that does not absolve anyone from following the direction given in General Comment No. 1 by the Committee on the Rights of Persons with Disabilities to work on the best interpretation of such persons' will and preferences. But it is an honest way of working, in the sense of being truthful and reflecting the kind of relations forged with persons with severe intellectual and multiple disabilities.

Note

1 Excerpt taken from p. 151 of M. C. Dunn, I. C. Clare and A. J. Holland, 2010. Living 'a life like ours': Support workers' accounts of substitute decision-making in residential care homes for adults with intellectual disabilities. *Journal of Intellectual Disability Research*, 54(2), pp. 144–160. Used with permission from John Wiley & Sons.

9

NOELLE PENS A POEM ABOUT HERSELF

Me

Half moon –
I think about me
being whole.

Friends cheer me up
When I am sad.
If I didn't have
Friends
Like the
Friends
I have now,
I wouldn't know
How to Get along in
Life.
Doran (2014)[1]

Noelle Doran's poem, 'Me', reproduced above, features in an anthology of poems and paintings published by the National Institute for Intellectual Disability, based at Trinity College Dublin, Ireland. The poem is paired, on the opposite page, with a painting by Karen Holland titled *Sad moon*, which features a red crescent moon surrounded by irregular circles, rather like misshapen moons.

DOI: 10.4324/9781003561644-9

The moon is only alluded to once in Noelle's poem but, since this mention is in the opening line, it becomes a reference point. In the opening stanza, written in bold, Noelle immediately likens herself to the moon, more precisely to a half moon thinking about herself being whole. The starting point then is Noelle feeling that there is something missing in her life, a state which – as we read in the second line of the second stanza – makes her feel sad. This sense of sadness and the analogy with the phases of the moon are reinforced by Karen Holland's painting.

Noelle's thinking about herself being whole is, by extension, linked to the full moon. When the moon goes through its phases – as it waxes from new to crescent to half to gibbous to full, and wanes back to the next new moon – it is of course still there. It is just that its position in relation to the sun and the earth obscures part, all or none of it. Likewise, Noelle's wholeness is always there; she is never partially a person. But her awareness of her wholeness waxes or wanes in tandem with how she is feeling. At the time of writing the poem, she seems to have been sad and feeling like a half moon, thinking about the possibility of being whole through her friendships.

The second stanza is entirely focused on how Noelle's friends make her feel, the positive effect they have on her and the vital role they play in her life. The moon analogy is implicit in these lines – the half-moonlike sadness experienced by Noelle can be transferred into a full-moonlike wholeness through her friends. Most likely, there are other people who have a significant presence in Noelle's life, not only her friends. There may be family, colleagues, professionals and other persons with whom Noelle has close and lasting relationships. But it is her friends who she mentions in this poem that she has penned about herself. It is they who ensure that no part of herself is occluded.

Noelle's focus on her friends highlights how friendship is a very particular type of relationship. It is neither dependent on blood relations nor on formal arrangements. We choose our friends from among the people we have contact with; but it is a choice freely made, unlike relationships formed with people who happen to be family members, or our neighbours, colleagues or providers of services that we use. Moreover, friendship involves deeply formed ties between persons, without the intimacy entailed in sexual relationships. Friendship is also assumed to be mutual and reciprocal. Helm (2021) relates friendship to the Greek word *philia*, which refers to the kind of love that reacts to positive qualities in another person. Noelle's feeling of wholeness can be seen as coming from her friends reacting positively to her and making her feel valued as a person.

Aristotle's perspectives on friendship are very often the starting point of philosophical discussions on the subject, including contemporary ones. As Sandra Schmidt Bunkers (2021) explains, for Aristotle friendship involves caring for others for their own sake, rather than because of any direct benefit for oneself. Bunkers' exploration of different perspectives on friendship can be summarised in her statement that it involves 'mutuality, respect, care, compassion, openness to the future, transformation, and intimate affiliations' (p. 110). These qualities of friendship are evoked in Noelle's poem as one can easily imagine that they enable her to feel whole.

Discussions of friendship in the twenty-first century cannot ignore the online connections and 'friends' created through social media. Although Noelle does not specify whether it is friendships in the virtual or the real world that cheer her up and make her feel whole, it is on the latter type that this discussion of her poem rests. It is through strong relationships formed with people one meets physically and with people one gets to know well that friendships like the ones evoked in the poem can be formed. How and to what extent such relationships can and do develop into friendships is the subject of much debate. For example, Phelan (2019) cautions against restrictive understandings of friendship, including Aristotelian notions of hierarchies of friendship and ideas about what constitutes a true friendship. Keller (2023) quips about how philosophical work idealises friendship, to the extent of making one feel bad about one's friendships that can never reach such ideals. He advocates for a broad understanding of how friendship is construed and what can be considered a good, better or best friendship. It depends, Keller argues, on 'the distinguishing needs, interests, and circumstances of the friends' (p. 561). It could be said that Noelle herself is idealizing her friendships by presenting them as the one thing that can make her feel whole. On the other hand, the effect on her that she mentions is simple enough – they cheer her up when she is sad.

While Keller (2023) deliberately moves away from a prescriptive view of friendship, he does identify three characteristics. Friendships, he writes, entail mutual concern for each other, enjoying shared activities and having trust in one another to a very high degree. Noelle's friendships might very well have these characteristics. There does seem to be a deep sense of trust. Noelle does not only feel it is safe to show her vulnerability, her sadness and feeling like a half moon to her friends. She also trusts them to support her to overcome this sadness and vulnerability.

We do not know who Noelle's friends are, but there is literature that sheds light on the friendship experiences of persons with intellectual disability and their perspectives on friendship. Jackson et al. (2024) reviewed seven research papers on the topic, and found that the qualities highlighted by the various participants with intellectual disability seem to fit well with the ways in which friendship is usually conceived – there is reciprocity, mutual help and trust. In the research reviewed by these authors, as well as in studies by Witsø and Hauger (2020), among others, persons with intellectual disability identify different types of persons as their friends, including other persons with intellectual disability, family members, neighbours, colleagues and those who work with them in service provision.

Identifying these persons as friends confounds ideas about friendship being a special relationship, apart from one's relations with relatives and from the relations built in the workplace and in other contexts. Adults with intellectual disability tend to spend their time in structured environments, especially within the home and service settings, with few opportunities to engage in informal activities in community settings. Josol et al. (2023) note the difficulties in the area of friendships of persons with intellectual disability: the tendency for them to make friends from within the family or service providers; the lack of reciprocity and mutuality in such friendships; and interpersonal issues such as communication or behavioural difficulties. When it comes to considering staff providing services as friends, there are also issues of boundaries that the staff are obliged to maintain. Similar findings are reported in the systematic review by Zambri et al. (2023).

McConkey and Lorenzo (2022) comment on how many persons with intellectual disability 'lead lonely and unfulfilled lives' (p. 381). They may be lonely not in the sense of being by themselves, but in the sense of not having relationships that afford possibilities for establishing deep connections which can evolve into friendships. For such connections to happen, the authors argue that persons with intellectual disability need to have more opportunities for active leisure pursuits in community settings. This point relates to one of the basic characteristics of friendship identified by Keller (2023), engaging in shared activities. The sense of fulfilment created through friendship also connects with Noelle's half-moon versus whole-moon image.

Persons with intellectual disability may need support to enjoy these pursuits and the possibilities they can make happen. There are persons with intellectual disability who have opportunities to form friendships; but they tend to experience them in specific environments where they enjoy what Power and Bartlett (2018) call 'moments of inclusion' (p. 562), rather than having a range of possibilities on a par with other adults. Very often, it is only from the limited possibilities available to them that persons with intellectual disability can develop friendships. Given all these limitations, it is not surprising that they may identify as their friends people who make them feel good about themselves, without actually being their friends.

This point, of course, also applies to Noelle. While we do not know who her friends are and how they became her friends, her poem hints at a past when she did not have such good friends, ones that made her feel whole. Lines 5 to 7 in the second stanza – 'Like the/Friends/I have now' – suggest that it is in the present that Noelle has friends to wax lyrical about. The word 'now', in particular, implies a contrast with a 'then' when she did not have these friends. This would mean that Noelle is in a good position to compare various relationships that had or did not have an element of friendship, to distinguish between them and to identify the best ones. Following Keller's (2023) argument, referred to above, we can see how Noelle applies her own criterion for discerning the most prized friends, the ones who cheer her up when she is sad and who make her feel whole.

Josol et al. (2023) note that the benefits of friendship for persons with intellectual disability are the same as for anyone else. They present their own research, which sheds light on how persons without intellectual disability perceive their friendships with those who have intellectual or developmental disabilities. The themes identified show that these friendships have the same qualities as those of others – they are mutually beneficial and include engaging in informal activities together, and sustained communication is identified as a key factor in maintaining the friendship. Mutual friendships, therefore, can happen for persons with intellectual disability; but they do not happen as often as they do for those without an intellectual disability. Reinders (2008) tells of his friendship with Ronald, a person with intellectual disability. He comments on people's surprise when he refers to Ronald as his friend as they assume that one cannot befriend someone who is so very unlike oneself. Reinders uses his account of his friendship with Ronald as a springboard for his book-length discussion on friendship with persons who have profound intellectual disability. These, he argues, can be the deepest friendships because they rely purely on accepting a person as they are, rather than for what they are able to do.

The reciprocity in Reinders' friendship and in the friendships of the participants in Josol et al.'s research is an important factor. Friendship cannot be a one-way thing. It is also largely an informal affair, and not one that can be legislated for. Tellingly, there is no legal article – in the 2006 Convention on the Rights of Persons with Disabilities (CRPD) or in any other disability anti-discrimination legislation – that provides a specific right to friendship. Article 23 (Respect for home and the family) asserts the rights of persons with disability 'relating to marriage, family, parenthood and relationships' (para. 1), but the relationships referred to there are sexual relationships. The assertion of these rights is important for persons with intellectual disability, given that this is an area where they generally encounter many obstacles (Pérez-Curiel et al. 2023). If sexual relations develop far enough for a couple to want to commit to each other in the long term, some kind of formal arrangement is likely to be put in place – marriage perhaps, or at the very least a contract for a place for the couple to live in. For friendships, there is never a specific need for such agreements. A couple of friends might decide to share a house or apartment, but such an arrangement is not a necessity for the friendship to flourish.

What can be achieved, through implementation of the CRPD, is the creation of the conditions necessary for friendship to flourish. Article 19 (Living independently in the community) and Article 30 (Participation in cultural life, recreation, leisure and sport) are particularly relevant in this regard. They require the removal of obstacles that prevent persons with disabilities from accessing community-based activities and the creation of disability-inclusive community environments. These requirements are in line with the argument proposed by McConkey and Lorenzo (2022), cited above, that the right conditions must be purposely created for persons with intellectual disability to form friendships. The right conditions include: possibilities for persons to be physically part of community-based leisure and other activities; provision of any support they need to go to these activities and take an active part; and the creation of welcoming environments in which they are not judged, made fun of or worse.

Having these conditions in place can enable friendships like the ones celebrated in Noelle's poem to flourish. The interplay between the formalities of creating such conditions and the informality of the friendships that they can make possible cannot escape our attention. It is an interplay that can seem contradictory. The qualities of friendship, discussed briefly above, entail a person using their personal agency to choose their friends and what activities they do together. More importantly, they entail a person choosing who to trust with what and how much. Such choices cannot be scripted and much less enforced. They need to spring from the person's exercise of their autonomy. For the nurturing of friendships that are as meaningful as Noelle's friendships are for her, there need to be choices which are freely made and freely acted upon. Such freedom suggests the need for informal arrangements in which autonomy can be exercised.

The formality of purposely creating conditions for friendships of persons with intellectual disability to flourish informally is far from being a contradiction, however. Given their support needs and the stigma and even hostility that they often encounter (McConkey and Lorenzo 2022; Power and Bartlett 2018), making deliberate arrangements for access to inclusive community-based activities can very well be a prerequisite for such friendships to flourish. These arrangements can even have friendship as a direct aim, such as in the case of befriending schemes (Brand et al. 2024). Some of the participants in the research by Josol et al. (2023) made friends with persons with intellectual disability through such schemes. Therefore, once again we see how formal arrangements can be key to the start of friendships that, like Noelle's, make a person feel whole. These friendships can then further reinforce participation in the community and a sense of belonging to it (Vuk 2023).

A crucial aspect of Noelle's friendships that she writes about in her poem is the direction and guidance they provide her. The last lines of the poem, 'How to Get along in/Life', read like the title of a self-help book. For Noelle, the guidance comes from her friends rather than a book. Without them she 'wouldn't know' how to go through the different phases of her life, the different circumstances and the different moods they give rise to.

Noelle's analogy of the phases of the moon is a very effective image for the reader to understand how she feels about her friends and how she would feel without them. However, like all analogies, the comparison breaks down at some point. The moon's phases are entirely predictable. They depend on its immutable relationship with the earth and the sun, and the fixed patterns of its own and the earth's orbit. Human relationships are far from predictable. It is not possible to know in advance when Noelle will need her friends to cheer her up, to guide her on how to get along in life and to make her feel whole. Furthermore, unlike the moon, Noelle can act spontaneously and autonomously. But the conditions around her need to be right for her to do so affirmatively. Taking deliberate action to create accessible and inclusive community-based activities and to provide any required support is an important step towards creating such conditions.

Despite the inevitable limitations of the moon analogy, there is one other way in which it works really well. The moon does not emit its own light – it depends on the sun to shine, and it depends on its position in relation to the sun and the earth for it to be seen from our planet. This image of the moon's dependency on others makes for a fitting comparison with human beings' dependence on each other. The value we give to friendships is an expression of this interdependence. Our friends are the people we have relationships with out of our own will, unlike the relationships we are obliged to have with family and co-workers, and those that are formed with people who provide us with services we need. As Noelle shows us, in her poem of just 36 words, friends enable us to think of ourselves as 'being whole'.

Note

1 Poem by Noelle Doran, 'Me'. In *Pen & Palette: A selection of poetry and paintings by students of the National Institute for Intellectual Disability, Trinity College Dublin*, p. 18. Used with permission of the National Institute for Intellectual Disability and Noelle Doran.

10

LEON CARRIES SOME BOXES

> [A] couple of days later I happened to be at a meeting when my mobile rang. [. . .] I ran downstairs and found Leon lying face down on the floor with his head inside a large cardboard box. He was . . . doing his best to knock over a pile of neatly stacked boxes. He was definitely succeeding in his intent. [. . .] The corridor now looked as if a tornado had just swept past . . .
>
> Gordon was standing a few steps away, keeping safe. Luckily, there was nobody else [there] at the moment so we were saved the usual litany of well-meaning but useless advice.
>
> I called Leon a couple of times, but he did not budge. Instead he tried kicking me, missing only by a hair's breadth. I went near Gordon and decided to wait there till the storm subsided.
>
> [. . .]
>
> We must have been standing there, listless, for more than half an hour when two caretakers arrived. They came in from the side door so they did not notice Leon, who was mostly hidden behind the boxes. They started moving the larger boxes, carrying them outside to be collected.
>
> Leon heard the activity and peeped out from his hiding place probably out of curiosity. One of the caretakers saw him and said hello. He asked him if he wanted to help.
>
> [. . .] Leon stood up and started carrying the boxes outside as if nothing had happened. The storm had passed!
>
> Abela (2012, pp. 44–45)[1]

This excerpt is taken from Marika Abela's research carried out in the secondary school in Malta where, at the time, she was working as an Inclusion Coordinator. For her research, for the Masters degree in inclusive education that she was reading for at the same time, Abela focused on four boys

DOI: 10.4324/9781003561644-10

with disability whom she was following, among them Leon. It should be noted that, at the time, Malta's state secondary schools were split into boys' and girls' schools, but they have since become co-educational. When the research was carried out, Leon was in his first year of secondary school and, Abela tells us, he was finding it hard to adjust to the new school. He has Down syndrome. He has difficulties with being understood when engaging in conversation.

Abela created four narratives from her data, using the techniques of creative nonfiction. Leon's narrative, from which the excerpt is taken, is titled 'Naughty n' Nice'. The narrative immediately places us in Leon's situation with the opening scene describing an incident where Leon was venting his frustration in a school corridor, kicking the locker and verbally attacking the assistant head who was trying to calm him down. The narrative then switches to a completely different scene with Leon working with his learning support assistant, Gordon, and Abela in a separate room from his classmates. They had a maths worksheet, which Leon wanted Abela to work on instead of him. While she worked her way out loud through the exercise, Leon became interested in what she was doing and ended up doing the work himself. The narrative continues with scenes of Leon's outbursts alternating with scenes of him contentedly working and cooperating with his educators.

The opening excerpt is one of the final scenes presented. The incident happened a couple of days after Abela had observed Leon working with Gordon in his classroom on a handout that his teacher had given him and proudly returning the completed work to the teacher. The contrast with the scene described in the excerpt is stark, and a vivid illustration of what Abela describes as Leon's 'rollercoaster behaviour' (p. 45). The same boy who is happy to do his schoolwork and, in another scene, play dominoes is also capable of creating tornado-like effects.

Whether the scene depicted in the narrative is one of cooperation or rebellion, it is always Leon who is at its heart, and it is in the same school that Leon engages in these very different behaviours. The environment is populated by fellow students, educators and other staff, all of whom impinge on Leon's behaviour and how he reacts to different stimuli. In this regard, there is much to be read in the school caretaker's invitation to Leon.

Before delving deeper into the interaction between Leon and the caretaker, it is worth looking at some other interactions between Leon and the people around him at school. The opening scene of Leon's narrative, described briefly above, depicts examples of unhelpful behaviour from those around Leon – for example, the assistant head whose attempts to calm him down served to agitate him further. In that scene, Abela also observes how, when students came out to watch after the end of their lesson, they gave Leon the attention he needed, motivating him to kick harder. In the excerpt quoted above, we get the sense that futile attempts at getting Leon to calm down were regular occurrences as Abela remarks how she and Gordon 'were saved the usual litany of well-meaning but useless advice'.

Given that direct intervention and advice about how to intervene directly were not proving to be of any use, the best course of action seemed to be non-intervention. In the scene portrayed in the excerpt, Abela finds Gordon standing by, at a safe distance. Her own short-lived attempt at intervening reminded her of the counteractive effect of getting directly involved in such situations. The best thing to do seemed to be to join Gordon in waiting for the tornado-like storm to subside. This approach certainly avoided provoking more excitement in Leon although, half an hour later, when the caretakers arrived, he was still alternating between bouts of kicking and periods of inactivity. Non-intervention was therefore only a partially successful approach. The first scene, as well as some others, ends with the school calling Leon's mother to pick him up. This tactic was a non-solution, however. Leon was effectively being excluded; and, for his mother, having to pick up her son from school on such occasions was a cause of frustration and heartbreak, as the narrative shows at a later juncture.

There was after all a way of directly interacting with Leon which, far from agitating him further and ending with him being sent home, calmed him down. What the caretaker managed to do was create an abrupt change in Leon's mood and, consequently, his behaviour. He was transformed into a boy who was only too willing to help with carrying the very boxes he had been so intent on destroying moments before. This particular scene starts very much like the other incidents centred on Leon's outbursts. But, unlike those scenes, it does not end with his mother having to pick him up. Instead, its ending is much more akin to those scenes where Leon is happily working on the tasks set for him. It is also similar to the scene, which Abela places at the very end of the narrative, where she watched him play football, with the other boys not minding that he did not know which direction he should be running and which direction he should aim his goals at. That scene is itself a far cry from the one that inspired the title of the research article by Hodge and Runswick-Cole (2013), in which one of the boys with physical disability complained that his friends 'never pass me the ball' when they are playing (p. 311).

Abela reflects that what the boys playing football had done was to find a way 'to reach in to him and meet him on his own terms' (p. 46). This is also what the caretaker does. The suddenness with which Leon's behaviour is transformed is truly remarkable, and all at the behest of a question – asking him if he would like to help. That is a question that makes him feel valued, accepted as he is. Unlike the advice doled out to Abela and Gordon, which is well-meaning and useless in equal measure, the caretaker's question does not start from a position of judgement. The assistant head's entreaties in the opening scene of the narrative, Abela's own futile effort to engage with Leon in the excerpt above and similar attempted interactions with him call out his behaviour single it out as the problem and the cause of the difficulties experienced by Leon, his parents and his educators. On the other hand, the football match, Abela herself only indirectly inviting Leon to work on the maths exercises and the caretaker's question have a different characteristic in common – rather than being based on trying to shape Leon into an already formed mould of what a student in a mainstream secondary school should be like, they are based on an already formed acceptance of Leon as he is.

However, accepting Leon on his own terms does not mean condoning his destructive behaviour. Kicking lockers and tearing up boxes damages much more than these physical objects themselves. Such behaviour can destroy any chance for Leon to have constructive relationships with his schoolmates, his educators, his family and others around him. It obstructs the possibility of communication by and with Leon that allows for mutual exchange of information which is intelligible for him and those communicating with him, and on which further exchanges and communication can proceed and relationships can develop.

Leon's meltdowns preclude the possibility of such exchanges. By the time the incident narrated in the extract discussed in this chapter occurred, Abela knew better than to try to engage with Leon during the episode itself. After just two attempts, she stopped. Previous experience had already shown how such attempts only energised Leon, rather than calming him down. Abela and Gordon were waiting for this calming to happen so that they could interact with Leon again, in ways that allowed for mutual exchange and relationship-building, ways that they knew were possible.

But the caretaker did not have to wait for Leon's storm to subside to be able to have a mutual exchange with him. They connected with a simple question. Just by asking Leon if he wanted to help carry the boxes, the caretaker enabled him to transform his behaviour. From the target of Leon's frustration, the boxes became the means through which he could connect with the caretaker.

In fact, it was not only Leon's behaviour that changed, but also his mode of communication. Tony Osgood's (2019) book on how to support children and adults with intellectual disability or autism who have behavioural difficulties is also a book about communication. He discusses the central role that communication plays in our lives, and how vital it is for us to be able to have flourishing relationships. Furthermore, he argues that, for children who have cognitive difficulties and difficulties in verbal communication, acquiring skills to communicate constructively is not an easy accomplishment, partly because of their own difficulties and partly because of the failure of others to find ways of enabling them to develop these skills. They therefore use their behaviour to communicate, and when it is physical or psychological pain that they want to communicate, it is behaviour which others find challenging that they resort to. Abela leads the narrative to the incident in the extract with an observation about her belief that 'Leon was capable of showing dissent without resorting to extreme measures if shown how' (p. 44). This observation encapsulates the importance of seeing challenging behaviour as a mode of communication that needs to be replaced with more fruitful and much less destructive modes. In Leon's case, it is the caretaker who shows the way.

Earlier on in the narrative, Leon is described as having difficulty adapting to his new school. The transition from primary to secondary school can be daunting for many students, with or without disabilities (Van Rens et al. 2019). For Leon, it was proving overwhelming, and, being unable to express himself verbally in ways that could be readily understood by others, he was venting his frustration through episodes of behaviour that his educators were finding difficult to handle. They, too, needed to adapt to Leon. They needed to find ways of putting into practice Article 24.2(e) (Education) of the Convention on the Rights of Persons with Disabilities (2006) so that '[e]ffective individualized support measures are provided in environments that maximize academic and social development, consistent with the goal of full inclusion'.

In its simplicity, the caretaker's question shows what inclusive education, and inclusion more generally, is about. It is the school that needed to adapt, to cater for Leon's learning needs as well as his psycho-emotional needs. Leon's educators needed to find a way of connecting with him on his own terms, to make sure that he could connect with staff and students in the school, build wholesome relationships with them and learn serenely alongside his peers. Osgood (2019) discusses how communication is not only about expressing one's views and articulating one's needs. Communication, he states, is also 'a transmission of self' (p. 46). Denying Leon, and other children with disability who like him experience difficulties in making themselves understood, the means to develop effective communication skills is bound to have a deleterious effect on their development during their crucial formative years. Including Leon in his school means finding ways of communicating effectively with him and of enabling him to develop effective communication skills too.

Abela's narrative about Leon, and the insights she derives from her and other people's encounters with him within the school, speak to what is at the heart of inclusive education. In his appraisal of Len Barton's work in the field of inclusive education, Slee (2012) notes three elements that stand out, all of which are also found in Leon's narrative. First of all, Slee singles out the importance that Barton gives to students' voices and the need for educators to have enough humility to recognise that they need to learn from their students. Leon's encounter with the caretaker and the insight that Abela derives about communicating with him on his own terms is a prime example of the workings of this humility.

Secondly, Slee highlights how Barton's work shows us that we need to consider inclusive education not only academically but also as a social act, and therefore attending to its relational aspect. The narrative that Abela constructed from her direct encounters with Leon and her observations of others' encounters with him is very much about relationality. We can see which approaches enable connections between Leon and his interlocutors and which ones end up reinforcing the communication barriers they are seeking to dismantle.

Lastly, Slee notes how Barton's work demonstrates the important link between activism and research. Abela does not refer to any activist aspect of her work. However, through her writing, for example in Leon's narrative, we can see how she stands up for the rights of the students with disability she was working with. Her final observation in Leon's narrative is about the need to 'reach in to him and meet him on his own terms' (p. 46). Her use of 'reach in to' is very interesting. She could have written 'reach out to' and the sentence would still have made sense. But the latter phrasal verb implies a person remaining where they are and trying to connect with another from that place. The verb that Abela uses implies a willingness to move from one's place and enter the world of the other to understand what support they need and how one can best provide it.

Furthermore, in the opening extract, Abela uses the idea of safety in two ways. While Leon was kicking the boxes, she kept her distance to keep herself physically safe. In the next sentence, she uses the idea in a different manner – being saved (and therefore also being safe from) 'the usual litany of well-meaning but useless advice'. That advice was based on expectations for Leon to interact with others on their own preset terms. What was needed was for others to use Leon's own terms as a starting point, to venture out from their own comfort zone and reach in to Leon's own zone. There is enough in the narrative to show that this was possible, as noted earlier: Abela starting to work on the maths exercises herself rather than insisting with Leon that he does them himself; his schoolmates allowing him to play football as he saw fit rather than insisting that he follow time-honoured rules; and, finally, the caretaker asking Leon a question that transformed him into an equal communication partner rather than a boy whose wayward behaviour needed correction. At that moment, Leon was not just carrying some boxes; he was also carrying a powerful message about the need to adapt all aspects of school life if education is to be truly inclusive of all. This message, which Abela eventually works out, does not come from Leon's interactions with highly educated professionals. It comes from interactions with the school caretaker and some of his schoolmates who had the wisdom to intuit how to engage with Leon in non-judgemental ways that made him feel valued in a manner that was intelligible for him.

Note

1 Excerpt taken from pages 44–45 of Marika Abela, 2012. *The social inclusion of students with moderate to severe disabilities in a boys' comprehensive secondary school: A qualitative study*. Unpublished Masters Dissertation. University of Malta. Used with permission of the University of Malta and Marika Abela.

11

SOMEONE NEEDS AN EXPLANATION

> Well I was annoyed because I think that the barman just said 'sorry I can't serve you' and he didn't give (. . .) an explanation and I think that if anything ever happens where somebody is treating you unfairly that at the very least you need to find out and have an explanation and you know why is this happening (. . .). (Focus Group E)
>
> García Iriarte et al. (2104, p. 571)[1]

This quotation is from a participant in one of the focus groups held as part of the inclusive research project carried out by García Iriarte et al. (2014) on the key concerns of persons with intellectual disability in Ireland. The themes elicited from the findings relate these concerns to issues regarding the opportunities (or lack of them) for persons with intellectual disability to be able to take decisions about their life, to have self-determination. The excerpt chosen for this chapter pinpoints a crucial aspect of self-determination – being informed about decisions taken that affect a person's life and having the reasons behind them explained.

The source of annoyance for the Focus Group E participant is not just the fact that they were not served by the barman, but that they were not even given an explanation as to why. Presumably, the barman's problem was to serve this person an alcoholic drink, and it is on this assumption that this chapter's argument is built. Other themes identified by the researchers in their study include friendships and intimate relationships, employment, enjoying leisure time, having money and having one's citizen rights respected, including for living arrangements. Similar concerns have been raised by other

DOI: 10.4324/9781003561644-11

researchers, including the contributors to Grant et al.'s (2010) edited collection and Merrells et al. (2019).

Compared to these concerns, the source of this participant's annoyance may seem inconsequential; but the encounter between the barman and the person with intellectual disability involved is based on fundamental issues that far outweigh any perceptions of triviality. After all, the participant links the incident to the issue of unfair treatment and the need for such situations to be explained.

We do not know how the barman came to the conclusion that he could not serve this person with intellectual disability. Did he make a snap decision on the basis of their appearance as someone with an intellectual disability? Was he informed in advance by someone else, perhaps a support worker or family member, that the person could not drink alcohol? Was the refusal based on a mistaken idea of persons with disabilities not being able to drink alcohol? Or was it based on valid medical and health reasons? And, if it was alcohol that was the problem, was the person given another option? We do not have the answers to these questions; but the most significant issue is that the person with intellectual disability themselves never got an answer either. In fact, that person does not seem to have had the opportunity to ask any questions in the first place.

This person's complaint about not receiving any explanation points to a crucial aspect of being able to live life on one's own terms, a key principle in the Convention on the Rights of Persons with Disabilities (CRPD 2006). In order to be able to make choices and decisions about one's life, one must have relevant information to hand, and explanations where that information is not clear. One of the most enduring images of the decision-making process is that of the ladder of participation, first devised by Sherry Arnstein in 1969 (republished as Arnstein 2019), which has since been adapted for use in different contexts. Writing in the context of empowering citizens, Arnstein (2019) places 'manipulation' on the bottom rung of the eight-step ladder and 'citizen control' at the top (p. 26). As Arnstein herself explains, the ladder is a simplification of how participation in decision-making happens. Nonetheless, it is a useful schema for conceptualising such participation as a process that can start small and grow into more direct and meaningful control over one's life.

In Arnstein's ladder, the first two rungs, 'Manipulation' and 'Therapy', are categorised as 'Non-participation'. The author uses therapy to refer to 'a masquerade of involving citizens in planning, the experts subject the citizens to clinical group therapy' (p. 27) – for example, inviting someone who makes a complaint to attend therapy sessions, rather than addressing the problems raised in the complaint. The former implicitly places the onus on the complainant to change their behaviour, while the latter validates how they feel about a particular situation. The next set of rungs – comprising

'Informing', 'Consultation' and 'Placation' – is labelled 'Degrees of tokenism'. It is significant that Arnstein refers to degrees of, rather than complete, tokenism. Indeed, if misused, these actions can easily be tokenistic. However, when used well – especially consultation and informing – they can be important steps towards the last set of three rungs. This set, labelled by Arnstein as 'Degrees of citizen power', comprises partnership, delegated power and, finally, citizen control. Just as with tokenism, Arnstein points to *degrees* of citizen power, rather than to having total control or nothing at all. Citizen control/power is also the last rung of the participation ladder and the other rungs are there to enable a person to reach it.

The complaint by the Focus Group E participant in Garcia Iríarte et al.'s (2014) research evinces that person's struggle to get to the upper reaches of this ladder. The situation that they describe can be correlated with Arnstein's second and third rungs, informing and consultation: 'you need to find out and have an explanation and you know why is this happening'. That the participant is complaining about the lack of information and explanation, and the lack of opportunity to obtain them, attests to the importance of these two rungs in Arnstein's ladder of participation, the risk of tokenism notwithstanding. Being able to find out *why* something is happening in their life is an important step towards a person with intellectual disability being able to make choices, to work in partnership with others, to share the power to take decisions with them and, ultimately, to feel in control of their lives.

Let us imagine that the barman had good reasons not to serve alcohol to this participant, for example because he had been informed they were on medication that does not mix well with alcohol. Let us then imagine that the person with intellectual disability received information about this, an explanation was given and, after a discussion, they agreed it would not be wise to take alcohol at the bar. Outwardly, the outcome would have been the same – the person would go to the bar and not be served alcohol. They might even still feel that not being able to buy alcohol is unfair and frustrating, however valid the reasons. What would be different would be the person's feeling about the interaction with the barman, as it would not leave them feeling helpless.

It is for this reason that the complaint about what failed to happen at the bar carries significance beyond the micro interaction – which probably lasted for under a minute –between the barman and the person with intellectual disability. The utterance from the barman as recalled by the participant – 'sorry I can't serve you' – is so brief that it does not place the person with intellectual disability anywhere near Arnstein's ladder of participation, not even on the first two rungs. That is, there is not even any pretence of involving the person in the decision to not serve them. The only information the person receives is that they cannot be served, which hardly counts as information at all. The 'sorry' at the start of the utterance, as reported by the focus group participant, could lend it an air of apology. It indicates that the barman was aware that his customer would not be pleased with not being served the drink they wanted. However, if there was the intention of an apology from the barman's side, the lack of explanation undermined it and the utterance comes across as more dismissive than apologetic.

The lack of explanation also undermined the social inclusion of the person with intellectual disability. The complaint made by the person in the focus group about their interaction with the barman – or rather the failure to have an interaction – highlights how inclusion is not only about persons with disability being physically present in mainstream community spaces. It is also about equitable treatment. Using Arnstein's ladder, we can see how a purportedly participatory act – being in a pub – became non-participatory for want of an explanation and information about why the person was not served.

Significantly, access to information is recognised as a right in the CRPD. It is mentioned in the Preamble, in the general obligations set out in Article 4, as an integral part of accessibility (Article 9), and in its own right as part of Article 21 (Freedom of expression and opinion, and access to information). The most widely used system to provide access to information for persons with intellectual disability is through the creation of easy-to-read documentation. There are guidelines on how to produce such documents, such as those published by Inclusion Europe (2009).

A significant aspect of easy-to-read information is that it is co-produced with persons with intellectual disability (McVilly et al. 2018). In fact, an important step in its production is to check it with persons with intellectual disability themselves to ensure that it is indeed easy to read. Such checking, however, cannot guarantee comprehension as the ability to understand written information – and to decipher it in the first place – varies among the target audience of easy-to-read texts. These texts therefore often need to be accompanied by explanations for people with intellectual disability to be able to benefit meaningfully from them (Callus and Cauchi 2020; Mander 2015). It is no wonder then that the Focus Group E participant mentions the need for an explanation, for answers to the 'why' question. The provision of easy-to-read information and of explanations of this information where necessary are important steps in ensuring persons with intellectual disability are involved in decisions affecting their lives, even if in themselves they are insufficient. In Arnstein's eight-rung ladder of participation, informing is placed on the third rung. It is a means to an end, with the ultimate aim being citizen power – that is, the last three rungs of the ladder, which represent partnership, delegated power and, finally, citizen control.

However, even if it is a means to an end, accessible information is important in and of itself for persons with intellectual disability. At one end, it can be used to provide explanations about an individual's specific health needs, such as in the speculative example provided above. At the other end, it can be used to inform persons with intellectual disability about their rights, to enable them to recognise discriminatory treatment and know what to do about it. For example, one of the aspects of discrimination included in Malta's UNCRPD Act (2021) is the failure 'to furnish information with regards to the rights of the other [i.e. disabled] persons by means of communication which the other person can understand' (Fourth Schedule, Article A(d)).

We do not have enough information from the opening quotation to ascertain whether and to what extent the barman's failure to serve the Focus Group E participant was itself discriminatory. The participant speaks about being treated 'unfairly', a word the *Oxford English Dictionary* defines as 'an unfair manner; inequitably, unjustly'. If either of the two scenarios set out above is correct, discrimination could have occurred: (a) if the barman simply assumed that a person with intellectual disability cannot drink alcohol; or (b) if there were valid reasons for not serving alcohol to this particular person – for example on medical grounds – but no explanation was provided. Being able to find out why this treatment occurred is identified by the participant as a basic need, a need that obviously goes beyond the one-to-one interaction with the barman and applies to all aspects of the lives of persons with intellectual disability.

However, even if this incident at the bar is taken as representative of the control exerted over the lives of persons with intellectual disability more generally, the ramifications of the barman's refusal to serve the Focus Group E participant, or to at least proffer an explanation, are also worth considering intrinsically. This is because going to a bar for a drink with others both promotes and indicates community inclusion. In fact, García Iriarte et al. (2014) quote research participants with intellectual disability in four other focus groups who raise complaints about not being able to enjoy this activity. For example, a participant in Group A describes as 'the lousiest thing' not being able to drink alcohol, just because some persons with intellectual disability cannot do so (p. 569); and the issue of not taking alcohol is raised by a participant in Group D in a different manner: 'we meet friends and we talk to them and have a few drinks, but not alcohol[ic] drinks' (p. 570) For this participant, taking non-alcoholic drinks seems to be uttered as a statement of fact, which they are fine with. A reason they might leave a pub, they say, is if they don't like the music.

Going to the pub is a means of not only meeting one's friends but also of intermingling with other persons who live in one's community, including those who do not have a disability. This aspect is brought up by a Focus Group D participant as well as one of the participants in Focus Group C, who reports that going to the pub on Tuesday night provides an opportunity 'to meet up with some of the locals' (p. 570). On the other hand, one of the Focus Group P participants complains about not being able to interact with other people: 'you say something to them, they ignore you straight away. People are very ignorant. (. . .) They don't answer you' (p. 572). Taken together, these quotations and the one opening this chapter highlight the importance that the persons with intellectual disability who are speaking attach to being able to meet up with friends in the pub on an equal basis with non-disabled people who use the pub as a means of enjoying themselves and being part of their own community.

The discussion of Focus Group E participant's encounter with the barman highlights the need for interactions between persons with and without intellectual disability to be based on a premise of equality, while attending to the support needs of those who do have intellectual disability, including in relation to providing information and explanation and leaving room for discussion. All that is needed for these interactions to be equitable is encapsulated in the quotations from García Iriarte et al.'s (2014) research presented here, especially the one opening this chapter. Going to the pub, enjoying time with one's friends, mixing with other people, striking up conversations with them and being served drinks (alcoholic or non-alcoholic) are all mentioned. The main complaints arise from experiences where there is a lack of communication, most notably the ignorant people mentioned by a Focus Group P participant and the lack of explanation complained about by the Focus Group E participant.

Tellingly, García Iriarte and her co-authors place the quotation from the latter in their discussion of self-advocacy. Self-advocacy is, first and foremost, about persons with intellectual disability speaking up for themselves (Sutcliffe and Simons 1993); but it is also about persons being supported speaking up for themselves, as the history of self-advocacy has shown (see, for example Buchanan and Walmsley 2006). In this context, being able to speak for oneself – with or without support – does not refer to assessing whether a person has the innate capacity to speak for themselves. That capacity is taken as a given. Instead, it refers to the person having the opportunity to speak for themself and creating the necessary conditions for them to do so.

These conditions obviously entail communication, which, in turn, involves the flow of information. Moreover, informing and explaining need to be reciprocal affairs. Focus Group E participant's statement that 'you need to find out' highlights the importance for persons with intellectual disability to have the opportunity to ask questions, to discuss with their interlocutors, to be able to show what information needs to be imparted and what needs to be explained. That process is also part of self-advocacy. Without communication, there can be no information, and certainly no explanation; and, without information and explanation, interactions cannot proceed on an equal footing.

At the most pragmatic level, the participant's need to know 'why is this happening' remains unaddressed. Their recollection of the encounter with the barman implies that there was no space for them to ask why they could not be served. The negativity of the memory of the encounter resonated deeply enough with this person for them to bring it up in the focus group they participated in. The barman's statement seems to have been final. A more open attitude, a disposition that welcomed questions and displayed the willingness to answer them, would have transformed the encounter into an opportunity for the person with intellectual disability to grow in their self-determination and to practise self-advocacy by being given relevant information about their life and the opportunity to ask questions and seek explanations.

Note

1 Excerpt taken from page 571 of Edurne García Iriarte, Patricia O'Brien, Roy McConkey, Marie Wolfe and Siobhain O'Doherty, 2014. Identifying the key concerns of Irish persons with intellectual disability. *Journal of Applied Research in Intellectual Disabilities*, 27(6), pp. 564–575. Used with permission from John Wiley & Sons.

12

BRIAN HAS IDEAS

SCENE [11]: DAVID DIRECTS MARK

David: [. . .] He's not listening. It's just because, ah, he keeps saying stuff about what we are doing and keeps coming up with these kind of, um, you know ethical problems and moral problems that we can't do this, we can't do that, and I just want you to be free. Yeah? You know the way Brian has written it don't feel you have to do it absolutely word for word. Just feel free to use it as a . . .

Brian: Script.

David: Ah . . .

Brian: A script.

David: Ah . . .

Brian: A script.

David: Springboard. Like in a swimming pool when you dive in. You know, it's like Brian has written the springboard but you are going to have to do the dive.

Brian: Don't be afraid to jump into it. Give it all you've got.

SCENE [13]: BRIAN HAS AN IDEA

Brian: I've just been thinking, why don't we make our characters more like comic characters? Make the villains more powerful than the heroes.

David: We've got what we need.

Brian: I'd just like to add something in it.

DOI: 10.4324/9781003561644-12

David: We are fixing now; we are fixing. If you want freedom you've got to make it fixed. I know that sounds contradictory but what I mean is, we need to feel secure. You've got to perform this. You're looking for excuses.
Brian: No, I'm looking for ideas.
David: No, you've got plenty of ideas. Stop trying to add ideas.[1]

These two scenes are from the play within a play of the Australian company Back to Back Theatre's *Ganesh Versus the Third Reich*, which was first staged in 2011. The play's main story is about the Hindu god Ganesh's mission to rescue the swastika from Hitler. The play within this play is a metanarrative about the discussions and rehearsals that led to the script for the main story to make *Ganesh Versus the Third Reich* itself. The scenes with these discussions take up more than half of the play. In this, its 25th production since it started out in 1987, the Back to Back Theatre ensemble wanted to draw the audience's attention to the play as much as to how it was made.

We cannot expect the dialogue in these 'meta' scenes, such as those reproduced above, to be taken word for word from what Back to Back members said to each other. In a chapter in the same book where the script appears, Prior (2013) describes how the company's work is created through improvisations that are recorded, transcribed, reviewed and then edited. It is in this way that the final script used in each performance is constructed. For *Ganesh Versus the Third Reich*, the ideas for the main plot developed from a neo-Nazi figure created by one of the company members and another member's interest in the Hindu god Ganesh (Gladwin and Gough 2013). The metanarrative plot was added as a means of showing how their rehearsals work. In the scenes related to this plot, the actors are performing a version of themselves (Prior 2013).

The two excerpts being discussed in this chapter present dialogue between David Woods, the only non-disabled member of the cast, and Brian Tilley, who has an intellectual disability, as do the other ensemble members. The two scenes from which the excerpts are taken are interspersed with a scene from the main story. In both, the discussion centres on the freedom that the actors can take with the script. In the second excerpt, David speaks about the need for freedom to be fixed, which he admits sounds contradictory. In fact, what he tells Brian here is at odds with what he tells him in the previous one.

In the first excerpt, and in the whole scene, the dialogue is initiated by David. He wants to talk to Brian about fellow actor Scott Price's complaints about the script and how they are hampering their freedom. Using the figure of Ganesh risked Back to Back Theatre being accused of cultural appropriation. Besides, a story about Hitler is of course always a rather risky venture. David emphasises the need for the actors to be free, to use the script as a springboard from which to dive. David is very much in control of the dialogue in the whole scene. When he pauses to search for the word he wants to use, he does not accept Brian's suggestion of 'script', and at the end Brian articulates what David had just told him in different words. In the second excerpt and the scene from which it is taken, it is Brian who initiates the dialogue. However, despite this reversal of roles, it is still David who controls the dialogue. Brian's new idea for the script is shot down by David. Together, these two scenes make one wonder just how much influence the ensemble members with intellectual disability are able to have on Back to Back Theatre's production.

However, what may at first appear to be only a tokenistic participation of persons with intellectual disability in performance theatre is actually a response to the idea of persons with intellectual disability only being involved in performance theatre (or other activities) in a tokenistic manner. Brian and the other actors are as deeply involved in these scenes as they are in the rest of the play, and in other Back to Back Theatre productions. In the scene in which Brian is apparently being told what to do by David, in which David seems to be the one calling the shots and setting parameters of freedom for Brian and the other actors, the latter are very much playing an active part. They are an integral part of the group of people who have contributed directly to the process of creating the script for the play in which, at least in these scenes, they play actors who seem to be told what to do under the guise of having the freedom to be directly involved in the production.

The perceived tokenism that the company's performers are reacting to here is encapsulated in an incident that happened in 2009 in Belgium, where Back to Back Theatre was performing *Food Court*, the production that preceded *Ganesh Versus the Third Reich*. This incident is referred to by Prior, among others, in *We're People Who Do Shows*:

> A man in the audience stood up and threw a metaphorical grenade into the room. 'I don't believe these people made this work,' he said. 'I have worked with people like this and I don't think they are capable of it.' One of the actors, Scott Price, livid at the presumption, stood, up, grabbed the microphone and said: 'Well mate, you can just get out of here because what you just said is so wrong and so offensive.'
>
> *(cited in Prior 2013, p. 211)*

Taking this context into account, the presentation of David as the domineering, non-disabled person is ironic and a dig at those who, like the audience member in Belgium, judged the performance on the basis of their own presumptions. The irony takes on additional resonance because of the self-referential nature of these two scenes. Brian, Scott and Mark who all feature in Scene 11, are sending up presumptions of incompetence not by showing their ability to suggest new ideas and influence the production process directly – which they do in other scenes from the metanarrative – but by pretending to be manipulated by David. It is the *pretending* that is key here, especially because it is so sophisticated. Brian, Scott and Mark are actors with intellectual disability in real life. In these two scenes, they are on stage pretending to be actors with intellectual disability called Brian, Scott and Mark who are being ordered around by David, a non-disabled actor who is pretending to be David, a non-disabled director who sets out the limits of freedom afforded to the disabled actors. The irony is that Brian, Scott and Mark know that they are pretending to be unknowingly manipulated.

The awareness of pretence by these three actors and by Simon, another cast member, is discussed later in Scene 17 when Scott calls into question Mark's ability to distinguish between the pretence on stage and real life. While the scene is based on a real exchange between the actors during rehearsal, here Mark is also knowingly pretending to be an actor called Mark whose ability to tell fiction from reality is doubtful.

The metanarrative scenes in the play do not just provide a glimpse into the collaborative ways in which Back to Back Theatre's productions develop. They also provide a parodic commentary on the attitudes of those who doubt the ability of the actors with intellectual disability to contribute in such a proactive manner. Later, David refers to the 'empty seats' which will have people in them 'when the show is on', further heightening the self-referential nature of the metanarrative scenes. The seats, of course, are not empty at all. The whole scene is being acted in front of an audience. In fact, the promotional video of *Ganesh Versus the Third Reich* (Back to Back Theatre 2009) features part of this scene, including appreciative laughter from the audience.

Collaboration in the development of scripts involving performers with intellectual disability is a model that is used by other organisations as well, such as the Malta-based Opening Doors Association (n.d.), which in 2018 published a collection of essays by people involved with the organisation. For example, in her discussion of Opening Doors' choreographic practice, artistic director Ilona Baldacchino (2018) presents what she calls the 'adaptive facilitation model', which provides a structure and at the same time is 'flexible enough to be altered' (p. 120). Likewise, its music leader, Luke Baldacchino (2018), describes how the members of the music groups are directly involved in the development of group performances, which also include solo performances from which 'the uniqueness of each individual' emerges (p. 85). Finally, Lou Ghirlando (2018, p. 107) describes how those supporting the theatre group's members keep their 'eyes, minds, hearts and ears' open to themes emerging in the improvisations created by the performers with intellectual disability, eventually intervening by reminding them of the improvisations that they kept returning to and encouraging them to explore them further, and even reinforcing them by introducing props inspired by these recurring scenes. These are also ways in which Article 30 (Participation in cultural life, recreation, leisure and sport) of the Convention on the Rights of Persons with Disabilities (2006) can be realised for many persons with intellectual disability.

The processes described by all three authors in the Opening Doors anthology point to structures devised by performers who do not have a disability to enable performers who have an intellectual disability to express themselves through their chosen genre, develop their performance skills and put on shows. The non-disabled persons bring their professional knowledge to bear in the way each work develops. In this regard, David's statement in Scene 13 – 'If you want freedom you've got to make it fixed' – is not as contradictory as it may seem to be at first. Indeed, Ghirlando's description almost mirrors what David tells Brian: at some point the improvisation needs to stop and the work on the performance itself to start.

Within the structures provided by groups such as Back to Back Theatre and Opening Doors, among many others, persons with intellectual disability can thrive. This is because, even if there are boundaries that define the structure, they are limits rather than limitations. Furthermore, they are there to guide the creative process rather than shackle it. Most importantly, they are structures created by non-disabled persons with expertise in the performing arts on the assumption that there is a creative process that can be engaged in with persons with intellectual disability. What they all bring to each performance and what is valued is the lived experience of having an intellectual disability and the experiential knowledge accrued from it (Borkman 1976). There is a crucial presupposition that this knowledge is not only valuable and relevant for the performance at hand, but also that those who hold it can share it meaningfully.

The comment by the audience member in Belgium is based on very different assumptions. He declared that he was speaking on the basis of his own work experience. The contrast between the collaborative processes described above and this person's comments highlights the double bind faced by many persons with intellectual disability. The cognitive impairment associated with intellectual disability requires the provision of structured support for those affected by it to thrive and develop. If the persons who work and live with them start with a presumption of incompetence, this support is not provided because it is considered to be unnecessary. As a result, persons with intellectual disability do not develop the abilities to express themselves, reflect on their lived experience and articulate the knowledge that arises from it. The presumption of incompetence is then confirmed, a confirmation that easily leads to the conclusion that 'these people' are not capable of engaging in collaborative work. No wonder then that Scott was livid.

Scott's outburst about the audience member's comment could just as easily have been expressed by the non-disabled members of Back to Back Theatre. The assumption that the performers with intellectual disability could not have made the work themselves sets the latter up as liars, misleadingly presenting the performance as something other than it is. They, too, are helpless in the face of this accusation, since it is grounded in deficit-based assumptions which they cannot easily debunk – whatever they say or do will be misinterpreted in terms of the presumed incompetence of the persons with intellectual disability they collaborate with. The difference of course is that, while these non-disabled persons have the option of leaving Back to Back Theatre and engaging in other work, the members who are labelled as having an intellectual disability do not have the option of setting their label aside.

What the cast of *Ganesh Versus the Third Reich* do, therefore, is challenge the mistaken assumptions often associated with having an intellectual disability. The two scenes from which the opening excerpts are taken, as well as some other scenes, project what it would have been like for David to take complete control of the process. Heated exchanges from the cut and thrust of the rehearsals are likely amplified to provide an ironic commentary on the assumption of incompetence. What appears to be the control of a group of performers with intellectual disability by a non-disabled director is actually the reverse, and the former are in on the joke.

The presumption of incompetence itself, from which persons with intellectual disability can have no appeal, is no joke at all. In *Ganesh Versus the Third Reich*, the main plot's focus on Hitler immediately brings to mind the Nazi's extermination programme, which started with persons with intellectual disability through the Aktion T4 euthanasia programme (Hepburn 2014) and its eugenicist ideas (Snyder and Mitchell 2010). The characters of Hitler and Joseph Mengele are played by actors with intellectual disability, which adds to the self-referential nature of the play. Mark (who plays Hitler) and Scott (who plays Mengele) are not just pretending to be non-disabled persons, but ones who hate persons with intellectual disability, such as Mark and Scott themselves, so much that they want to use them for experiments and to exterminate them.

The scenes containing the two excerpts present only one aspect of the complexity of *Ganesh Versus the Third Reich*, how it was made and the reasons for making it. It is an aspect that goes right to the heart of the collaboration between persons with and without intellectual disability. The type of collaboration under scrutiny in this chapter is based on the presumption that it is possible because different persons bring different qualities and different types of expertise to the table and that everyone's contribution can be fruitful if the right support structures are in place. These structures are needed for the collaboration to take shape. The 'fixed freedom' that David insists on in Scene 13 of the play can actually be enabling if the collaborative work is approached with a favourable disposition towards the abilities and competence of persons with intellectual disability.

In life, as on stage, what persons with intellectual disability need is to be active collaborators in planning processes that affect their lives. Just as in the work of Back to Back Theatre in Australia, Opening Doors Association in Malta and many similar ensembles, persons with intellectual disability should not have their lives scripted for them, but instead should be co-writers of their script. Taking a leaf from the book of organisations such as these means that professionals, family members and those who live and work with persons with intellectual disability discuss with the latter, and create spaces in which the latter can come up with ideas about what they would like to do and can articulate their wishes, needs and wants. These ideas and articulations can be adapted. What is important is that they form the basis of the script – or plan – for each person with intellectual disability. The only difference is that, unlike play scripts, which at some point need to be fixed and finalised (as David advises Brian), each plan needs to be continually revised to ensure that it is mainly the ideas that persons with intellectual disability have about how to lead their own lives that inform what goes on in those very lives.

Note

1 Excerpt taken from the script of *Ganesh Versus the Third Reich*, devised by Mark Deans, Marcia Ferguson, Bruce Gladwin, Nicki Holland, Simon Laherty, Sarah Mainwaring, Scott Price, Kate Sulan, Brian Tilley and David Woods. Published in 2013 in the Performance Research Books title *'We're people who do shows'. Back to Back Theatre: Performance, Politics, Visibility*, edited by Helena Grehan and Peter Eckersall. Used with permission of the publisher.

13

SHEA RECLAIMS HER VOTE

> I am now 31 years old, I, have Down syndrome and am an advocate for adults with Down Syndrome speaking to the community about disabilities, Inclusiveness and discrimination. With regards to your letter stating: that you believe I do not understand the nature and significance of enrolement [*sic*] and voting, I can assure you I most certainly do!
>
> I demand my right to vote and demand that I am placed back on the electoral role as I requested.[1]

Shea MacDonough wrote the letter from which this excerpt is taken as a reply to the Australian Electoral Commission (AEC), after it rejected her application to be put back on the electoral roll. She had been taken off the roll by her parents when she turned 18 as they felt that at the time she could not understand the electoral process and could come under undue influence. Shea's main motivation for re-inclusion on the electoral roll was to be able to vote for same-sex marriage, thus supporting her cousin who was in a same-sex relationship. Thrown into this situation are various factors, among them deeply embedded family ties, issues of citizenship and civil rights, the workings of specific electoral systems and outdated yet persistent misconceptions about the mental capacity of persons with intellectual disability.

Shea spent 13 years off the electoral register, and it is significant that what motivated her to reclaim her right to vote was the wish to support her cousin and her partner's relationship. This wish is testimony to the bond that Shea enjoys not only within her immediate family, but also with the extended family. Clearly, Shea understood the importance of supporting marriage for same-sex couples, and seems to have been particularly motivated because the issue directly affected someone with whom she had close ties. She also

DOI: 10.4324/9781003561644-13

understood the importance of advocating for their rights. After all, as she notes in her letter, she herself is a rights advocate on behalf of other persons with Down syndrome. Shea's appeal to the AEC links her capacity to do advocacy work by 'speaking to the community about disabilities, Inclusiveness and discrimination' with her capacity to 'understand the nature and significance of enrolement and voting'. The type of rights that persons with intellectual disability and those in same-sex relationships need to advocate for may be different, but the principle is the same: working for inclusiveness and against discrimination, which Shea mentioned in her letter.

However, this link between the two dimensions of rights is not reflected in the social and political context that forms the background to Shea's situation. It is a context which is open to reforming age-old concepts of who can be allowed to marry and widening these concepts to include same-sex relationships. But it is also the same context that holds on to age-old concepts about who should or should not be allowed to vote. The Australian Broadcasting Corporation (ABC) News article about Shea's fight to reclaim her voting rights from which the opening excerpt is taken quotes Natalie Wade, of Australian Lawyers for Human Rights, as referring to the law barring Shea, and many other persons with intellectual disability, from voting as being 'incredibly archaic'. It is not just that the terminology used is a throwback to older times, for example 'unsound mind' and 'incapable of understanding'. What is of greater concern is the blanket assumption that someone who has Down syndrome, like Shea, automatically lacks the mental capacity to play a meaningful part in the electoral process. As Carey (2009) notes, updating the terminology used in such laws is not enough if the prohibition on voting remains in place for persons with intellectual disability.

The dates of the events featured in the ABC News article are significant. The same-sex marriage issue was addressed in 2017 in a postal survey held by the Australian Parliament of people on the electoral register at the time (Australian Government Attorney-General's Department 2017). Shea's request to have her voting rights reinstated dates from that year. Although her reinstatement on the electoral roll came too late for Shea to support her cousin and others in same-sex relationships, she did eventually cast her vote in subsequent elections, including the federal election of 2022, when her letter featured in the news article. The significance of these dates emerges when they are put in the context of Australia having ratified the United Nations Convention on the Rights of Persons with Disabilities (CRPD) as far back as 2006.

The CRPD makes it clear that the rights entrenched in it belong to all persons with disability, since the text always refers to persons with disabilities, without mentioning the nature, degree or complexity of their impairments. Thus, the rights specified in Article 29 (Participation in public and political life) apply to all disabled persons. Participating in these processes includes the right to vote. This is a right which, historically, many disenfranchised people had to fight for – including poor people, women and members of ethnic minorities. As Altermark (2018) notes, the campaigns for these persons to vote were based on the argument that they had the mental capacity to do so, and that they could understand 'the nature and significance of enrolment and voting', to quote the law on which the AEC based its decision. This approach has worked to institute one-person-one-vote systems in countries that operate democratically. But, as Altermark also argues, it automatically excludes those who are not considered to have sufficient understanding to vote meaningfully, including many persons with intellectual disability.

This issue brings another CRPD item into the frame – Article 12 (Equal recognition before the law), which affirms that 'persons with disabilities enjoy legal capacity on an equal basis with others in all aspects of life' (para. 2). The General Comment issued by the Committee on the Rights of Persons with Disabilities (2014) on Article 12 laments the lack of understanding of what implementing it entails. This Comment provides an in-depth explanation of the requirements of Article 12, including: the importance of not conflating legal and mental capacity; of recognising that legal capacity is a fundamental human right; and of providing persons with reduced mental capacity the support and means to make decisions for themselves, including in exercising of their right to vote. The Comment also criticises traditional approaches to deciding whether a person has mental capacity, including the status approach – that is, basing the decision on a diagnosis, for example, of intellectual disability. This seems to have been the approach used by the AEC in their rejection of Shea's original application for re-registration.

The very existence of the General Comment on Article 12 evinces that the removal of legal capacity persists in many jurisdictions of countries that, like Australia, have ratified the CRPD. Shea's application to reclaim her vote dates from 2022, a full 14 years after Australia's ratification. At that stage, even if Shea's request had been accepted and she eventually regained her right to vote, many persons with intellectual disability in Australia were still disenfranchised on the basis of their status. They would not have been able to vote in the federal elections held that year, with some exceptions – such as Shea and 19-year-old Caitlin Woolley, who also campaigned for her right to vote, as mentioned in the ABC article.

The same disenfranchisement is experienced by many persons with intellectual disability worldwide. As Carey (2009) argues, the process of deinstitutionalisation may have enabled them to move into the community and to enjoy many rights, but they still do not enjoy full rights on an equal basis with other citizens in their own countries. Moving persons with disability out of institutions and into the community may have been partly based on the recognition that they do not pose a threat to that community, but the idea endures that allowing persons with reduced mental capacity to vote can threaten a community's democratic process.

The focus of campaigns for the rights of persons with intellectual disability, whether led by parents' organisations or by self-advocacy groups, has mostly been on access to education, employment and activities within the community. These are positive rights since governments are required to act for these rights to be realised (Centre for Constitutional Studies 2019). Enjoyment of these rights is essential for persons with intellectual disability to have a good quality of life and to be able to live independently. But, as Carey (2009) notes, 'surprisingly little attention was given to advancing access to negative liberties' (p. 169) – that is, those rights, including the right to vote, whose realisation depends on governments refraining from acting in order not to impinge on the individual's liberty.

In a video about her experience of reclaiming her vote, Shea remarks that 'Voting is the way to choose who will make important decisions that affect you: so we all have decisions made on our behalf and elect people to do so' (Inclusion Melbourne 2018). This observation says much about what is considered to be acceptable as direct or proxy decision-making in liberal democratic societies. Such societies set great store by the ability of adults to make day-to-day decisions and act on them on their own, as well as on their ability to decide who will represent them and have the authority to make political decisions on their behalf. They are therefore expected to act in a self-sufficient manner up to and including the point when they cast their vote. For them to be able to choose who will act and decide on their behalf in the political and legislative spheres they must first show that they can act and decide on their own. Persons with intellectual disability do not easily fit into this model: the fact that they often need support in making and enacting day-to-day decisions undermines their image as independent citizens, and consequently also their prospects of being seen as capable of voting. By not being allowed to vote, they have no say in who is elected and who legislates for or against restricting the very right to vote.

The logic of the disability rights movement, including the self-advocacy movement itself, is that not only is the need for support not a sign of dependence but that it is also the means through which disabled persons can achieve autonomy and independence. What is important is that the support is provided on terms set by the disabled persons themselves. This approach to independence is also the bedrock of the CRPD, whose first principles, found in General Principles, is 'Respect for inherent dignity, individual autonomy including the freedom to make one's own choices, and independence of persons' (Article 3a). Mention in various articles of the need to provide support, when needed, for a disabled person to exercise their rights bolsters the respect for their dignity, autonomy, freedom to make choices and independence. Among such examples is Article 29 (Participation in political and public life), which provides for 'allowing assistance in voting by a person of their own choice' (para. 29a(iii)). It is therefore the person themself who should choose who will assist them in voting, if they need anyone at all.

For Shea, there does not seem to be a need for assistance. She clearly knows her own mind and has the skills and experience to stand up for her rights. Other persons with intellectual disability might, however, need support that goes beyond someone marking the ballot paper on their behalf according to their own declared choices. This can happen, for instance, when a person does not have the use of their arms and needs someone to physically cast the vote for them or when a person with visual impairment cannot access the information on the ballot paper on their own. For persons with severe to profound intellectual disabilities, Martha Nussbaum (2009) suggested appointing guardians who vote on their behalf. This way, she contends, these persons are also represented when citizens go to the polls. She was aware of the controversial nature of her proposal and that there was little chance of it being approved. In fact, she presented it as a starting point for a debate on how to ensure the full recognition of political and civil rights of all persons with intellectual disability.

However, this is a debate that has yet to start. As it is, many electoral laws still seem to be wary of extending enfranchisement to persons with intellectual disability. Furthermore, contrary to the requirements of Article 12 of the CRPD, systems still often require these persons to prove they have the mental capacity to vote, rather than working on the assumption that they have this capacity unless proven otherwise. Shea was certainly the one who had to demonstrate that she had mental capacity. In having to do so, she experienced the exclusionary and discriminatory practices that she herself advocates against. She uses this advocacy work as evidence that she has the capacity to engage in the electoral process meaningfully and with understanding, in the letter she sent together with the medical report required by the AEC. Shea thus manages to reverse the situation by using the very same criteria on which her exclusion from the electoral roll was based.

Shea's advocacy work, in favour of the inclusion of persons with Down syndrome and of non-discrimination, not only shows she is capable of understanding what voting entails; it also shows she is capable of understanding the discrimination she was experiencing by having her original request rejected. Shea's letter of appeal turns that original request into a demand, one that was eventually heeded by the AEC. However, in the Inclusion Melbourne video (2018), she expresses her anger at not being enrolled when she first requested it and her unhappiness at missing out on expressing her views on the matter.

While the issues raised by Shea's experience reflect those encountered by many worldwide whose right to vote and to exercise other fundamental rights is taken away, there is an additional issue that arises from Australian's compulsory voting system: the right to vote is twinned with the obligatory duty to do so. As Evan Ekin-Smyth (from the AEC) is quoted as saying in the ABC News article, this obligation cannot be placed on someone 'who cannot, or can no longer, understand the nature and significance of enrolment and voting'. There is no option for someone to simply not turn up at the polling station or not submit their vote by post. A decision needs to be taken about each adult's capacity to vote.

The question is how to ensure that the right decision is made about a person's capacity to exercise their right to vote and that, in Carey's words, this right is not 'simply assumed away' (2009, p. 101). This is what seems to have happened with Shea's first request for reinstatement on the electoral roll. The AEC seems to have simply assumed that Shea's inability to vote with the requisite understanding at the age of 18 persisted as she grew older, as if having an intellectual disability precluded her from developing her skills and abilities in adulthood. Shea's letter hints at the inaccuracy of this assumption in the way she specified her age. The fact that she was 31 at the time of writing the letter was significant for her. At that age, one is a fully fledged adult, with adolescence far behind and the phase of one's youth reaching its end. Additionally, Shea emphasises that she is 'now' 31, implicitly contrasting her present level of maturity and understanding with how she was at the age of 18.

Australia's compulsory voting system notwithstanding, the situation is not necessarily any better for would-be voters with intellectual disability in other jurisdictions. Even in non-compulsory voting systems – which cover 85 per cent of countries where elections are held (International IDEA n.d.) – persons with intellectual disability often have their right to vote taken away. For example, in the European Union (EU), as the Fundamental Rights Agency (2024) reports, while many blanket restrictions on voting have been lifted, a significant number of hurdles to the right to vote still remain in place in many member states. According to the Agency, removing such restrictions is not only about not taking away a person's right to vote. Once that right has been established, it also involves enabling them to participate in the entire electoral process by, for instance, providing easy-to-read information – such as that provided by Down Syndrome Australia (2022).

Carey (2009) argues that rights are not just the statements made in legislation; they are also 'continually constructed and reconstructed both formally and in everyday practices' (p. 23). This relational perspective on rights brings into the frame the way that one's capacity to enjoy one's rights develops in the very exercise of these rights. Without the right to vote, persons with intellectual disability are not seen as needing access to information about the different aspects of the electoral process and about the issues that are most pertinent to each election. The lack of access to such information prevents persons with intellectual disability from developing the skills to exercise the right to vote on a par with other citizens.

The lack of parity with others is brought into sharp relief when contrasted with the importance given to people using their vote, for instance through compulsory voting systems (such as Australia's) or through promotional campaigns such as for the EU elections with the slogan 'Use your vote or others will decide for you' (European Parliament 2024). Without a vote, persons with intellectual disability have no option but to let others decide for them. With her vote, Shea (and other persons with intellectual disability) can contribute to the community to which she speaks in her advocacy work, and can help determine what kind of change happens in it.

Note

1 Excerpt taken from Shea MacDonough's letter in E. Wright and C. Edmonds, 13 May, 2022. An 'archaic' law has been removing Australians with disability from the electoral roll 'in droves', advocates say. ABC News. Available from https://www.abc.net.au/news/2022-05-14/disability-voting-laws/101059872. Used with permission from Shea McDonough.

14

RACHEL MOURNS HER GRANDFATHER

Researcher:	*You told me that you felt a bit, you felt quite sad, and that you miss him.*
Rachel:	*Yeah. I was, I got a bit worried.*
Researcher:	*You were worried?*
Rachel:	*I worried about him.*
Researcher:	*You worried about your granddad?*
Rachel:	*Yeah.*
Researcher:	*Do you know what you were worried about?*
Rachel:	*I'm a bit worried because I thought he's gone.*
Researcher:	*You were worried that he was gone?*
Rachel:	*Yeah.*
Researcher:	*And what was is about, what was it about that that made you worry?*
Rachel:	*It make me worry, it make me worried that I get, I get upset.*

Thorp et al. (2018, p. 49, italics in the original)[1]

This excerpt is from an interview with research participant Rachel, taken from Thorp, Stedmon and Lloyd's (2018) study of the experience of bereavement of four persons with intellectual disability. Rachel is speaking about mourning the loss of her grandfather. There are four different emotions mentioned in this part of the interview – feeling sad, missing him, being worried and getting upset.

This excerpt shows that there was considerable prompting from the researcher for Rachel to speak about the experience of losing her grandfather. Similar difficulties are also noted in the interviews with the other three

DOI: 10.4324/9781003561644-14

research participants. Earlier in the article, the authors explain that 'some prompts and probes were prepared and additional lines of questioning pursued to ensure that the participant was the "experiential expert"' (Thorp et al. 2018, p. 47). Speaking about one's experience of mourning and loss of close family members or friends can be difficult for anyone. The difficulties that Rachel experienced in articulating her emotions might as easily be attributed to this general difficulty as to the difficulties with articulation that are often associated with having an intellectual disability. The prompting by the interviewer is very prominent in this excerpt. In fact, the researcher speaks for almost two-thirds of the time, with Rachel's words taking up just over one-third of the text. It is of course what Rachel says that is the most important.

The excerpt opens with the researcher referring to what Rachel had mentioned earlier about feeling sad and missing her grandfather. The researcher steps gingerly into the matter, starting by qualifying the feeling of sadness with 'a bit' and then 'quite', thus gently escalating the degree of sadness evoked by Rachel's previous replies about missing her grandfather who has died.

Rachel agrees with the researcher's reference to the emotions she had previously mentioned, and then immediately introduces a new one: worry. Most of the rest of the conversation in this excerpt is about her worry. The researcher follows up with five questions, each one trying to delve into the nature of Rachel's worry. Her answers are mostly much shorter than the questions, with most of the conversational work thus being done by the researcher rather than by Rachel. However, even if there are so many prompts by the former, it is Rachel herself who is leading the conversation. The researcher's prompts are a good example of how one can understand what a person with intellectual disability is thinking and feeling with minimal input from that person, by allowing that person to provide the direction of the conversation.

The researcher's first question repeats Rachel's words in the interrogative form. It is as if confirmation is being sought that it is worry that Rachel wanted to mention, not another emotion. Rachel confirms this and adds information about the object of her worry – that she was worried about her grandfather. Once more the researcher repeats Rachel's words in the form of a question, perhaps once again to confirm that this is what she wanted to say. Rachel once again confirms. The researcher probes further into the matter. While worry is a natural emotion surrounding the death of a loved one, it is usually focused on the repercussions of that death on those who were close to the person who died, on a psycho-emotional as well as a practical level. However, Rachel declares herself to be worried about the person who died, her grandfather himself.

Next, the researcher nudges Rachel into articulating what it was that worried her about her dead grandfather. Her reply could be interpreted in two ways: Rachel is expressing worry about her grandfather himself, or she is referring to herself feeling worried when she thought about the loss of her grandfather and his absence in her life. What Rachel says next, after the researcher's further prompting, indicates that it is the second type of worry that she is referring to – that is, being worried about her own feelings, about being upset. Directly after this excerpt, the researchers also report that Rachel said: 'I feel very very sick when my granddad died.' Additionally, Rachel is later quoted as referring to her grandfather as being 'up, like a, like a heaven' (Thorp et al. 2018, pp. 49–50), thus further indicating that she is not necessarily worried about her grandfather himself but about how she feels about his loss.

Another aspect of interest is Rachel's switch from using the past tense to the present, midway through the excerpt. When the researcher asks her 'Do you know what you were worried about?', her reply does not start 'I was' but 'I'm'. And, even though the researcher's questions continue to use the past tense, Rachel's eventual answer, in the last line of the excerpt, is very much located in the here and now of the interview. Rachel is thus not only reflecting on how she felt when her grandfather died, but is also trying to articulate how she was feeling at the time the interview was held. Given that it is ordinarily much easier to articulate past emotions from which one has had time to distance oneself than present emotions that may still be too raw to process, Rachel's difficulty with expressing her emotions clearly is very understandable.

In the next section of their research article, Thorp et al. discuss the theme of a continuing relationship with the deceased relative that they elicited from the interviews. Here, the use of the present tense by the participants is noted. Rachel is quoted as saying: 'He is, he is a very nice man.' The researchers take this utterance to refer to an emotion suggesting 'that her grandfather continues to be experienced as "a very nice man" in her life' (2018, p. 49). This idea of the lost relative continuing to be present in the bereaved person's life is reflected in the article's title, 'I carry her in my heart' – a quotation taken from another participant, David, about his girlfriend. Rachel's mixture of emotions – being upset about the loss of her grandfather while simultaneously still experiencing his presence as 'a very nice man' – is also typical of the experience of grief. Thorp et al. refer to these apparently contradictory emotions as 'bittersweet', once again quoting Rachel: 'he loved me a lot, and (pause) I'd love a bit more of a time with my granddad' (p. 49).

As can be seen from this analysis, Rachel's experience of grief is unlikely to be very different from that of anyone else who has lost a much-loved person. Similar findings are reported by other researchers, including McRitchie et al. (2014), Read and Elliott (2003) and Ryan et al. (2011), with regard to persons with intellectual disability. These studies also show

how erroneous the assumption is that persons with intellectual disability quickly forget about their loss, as reported by Ryan et al. The similarity of these experiences of grief also highlights the importance of not pathologising the mourning process in persons with intellectual disability (Dodd et al. 2005). In fact, these experiences and emotions are very similar to those of anyone experiencing the loss of a person who was close to them. Death is a part of life; but it is also opposed to life, making it the most difficult of all parts of life. It marks a complete rupture in a relationship that can never be recovered. Even if the grieving person feels they still have a relationship with the one who has died, it can never be the same type of relationship.

The opening excerpt and the research by Thorp et al., as well as that of the other researchers more generally, show the need to attend to the support needs of persons with intellectual disability to process their grief. Unfortunately, at times not only are they not given this support, but they are also excluded from all processes surrounding the death of a loved one – from not being informed that the person is terminally ill to not attending the funeral (Read and Elliott 2003, Thorp et al. 2018).

Read and Wiese (2022) refer to Kenneth Doka's concept of disenfranchised grief – when a person's loss is not acknowledged and the person is unable to grieve alongside and in the presence of others. In their encyclopaedic summary of Doka's work on this concept, Bryant and Peck (2009) note that grief can be disenfranchised in various ways. For example, it happens when a person's relationship with the one who died is not acknowledged as having been meaningful enough to be mourned. It also happens when a person is not allowed to take part in public rituals of mourning and grief, such as funerals. And it happens when a person is not considered capable of feeling grief or when they grieve in an idiosyncratic way that does not conform with received and commonly held notions of what grieving behaviour is like. All these ways of disenfranchising grief are applicable to the experiences of many persons with intellectual disability.

Speaking of disenfranchised grief implies that one has a right to grieve, to mourn the loss of a loved one. This is not a right that is often written about, although there are discussions of it. For example, Minjee (2019) writes about her right, and that of fellow doctors, to grieve the death of their patients and of how this right is often not recognised. Hamer (2021) also writes about this right in relation to mourning relatives who die of cancer, insisting that there is no fixed way of grieving; it is a deeply personal process that needs to be acknowledged by those around the mourner. But there is no specific right to grieve, as Doka (2018) himself observes. Perhaps no one thought of articulating this right because mourning is such an inherent part of life and such an intuitive reaction to death that it is taken for granted. There is in fact no mention of the right to mourn and grieve in the Convention on the Rights of

Persons with Disabilities (2006) or any of the rights declarations and conventions mentioned in its Preamble.

Perhaps, also, grief is not seen as a right that needs to be upheld because it is an intensely private experience. But it is also a public experience, not only in terms of participating in public rituals of mourning but also in terms of the need to connect with others to share one's grief and process it. As McRitchie et al. (2014) note, exclusion from these processes creates additional loss as persons with intellectual disability are effectively excluded from the rituals and actions that help most people process their grief. Therefore, if there is differential treatment it needs to be in terms of the type of support offered to these persons to ensure that it caters for their impairment-related needs. Resources to provide such support include The Arc of the United States (2022), the UK charity Brake (n.d.) and Parks et al. (2014), as well as the story-telling approach advocated by Read and Wiese (2022).

Young et al. (2017) explore the grieving process in persons with profound intellectual and multiple disabilities (PIMD). Significantly, it is the carers' opinions that are sought – the difficulties with communicating directly and in depth with such persons through a research interview reflect the difficulties in establishing how they process the loss of a loved one. The carers' responses refer to both the cognitive and the emotional processing of grief by persons with PIMD. The latter are spoken of as demonstrating emotions related to the loss but not necessarily understanding what is happening. However, the lack of outward evidence of such understanding does not mean it is not there. It is more a question of the inability of those around the person with PIMD to understand how that person is internally processing the experience.

A vivid example of this process is provided by Nouwen (2022) in his account of the death of Adam, a person with profound disabilities whom he had befriended. Describing the reaction of the other residents of Adam's home, he mentions Rosie, who is non-verbal and uses a wheelchair. Nouwen says that Rosie seemed to live in her own world, never getting 'very close to people' (p. 95). But when the time came to go to the hospital to bid Adam a final farewell, Rosie wheeled herself to the hall, making it clear that she wanted to go to the hospital to be near Adam as he lay on his deathbed. Through that action, Rosie was also demonstrating that she was aware of what was going on, that she was attentive to the conversations and actions around her, and that she knew that Adam was extremely unwell and about to die. Nouwen describes how, once they were at the hospital, Rosie sat near Adam and held his hand while looking into his eyes. After around two minutes, she let go of his hand, gently laid it on the bed and leaned back. 'Rosie and Adam had said farewell to one another. Rosie was ready to leave' (p. 96).

Rosie's actions are not only a manifestation of how much she understood what was going on; they also show the close ties she had formed with Adam while they were living in the same home, despite seeming to others to be living in a world of her own. Rosie's story and Rachel's exchange with her interviewer in Thorp et al.'s study show how little we should take for granted when trying to comprehend the cognitive and emotional processes of persons with intellectual disability, especially if they have temporary or permanent difficulties with articulating their thoughts and feelings.

Furthermore, the various prompts by the researcher in the excerpt presented in this chapter show the value of sitting alongside a person with intellectual disability, conversing with them in order to understand what they are trying to articulate if, for one reason or another, words fail them. Sitting down and conversing with a person with intellectual disability in such a situation can entail prompting with questions, as the researcher does in the opening excerpt in order to understand what Rachel means when she says she worries about her grandfather. It can mean noticing intentional behaviours that are laden with a specific message, such as Rosie wheeling herself to the hall to show staff she wanted to bid Adam goodbye before he died. The details of such interactions will vary from person to person and from situation to situation, but they have a common denominator – recognising a priori that the person with intellectual disability has something of value to say about the loss of a dearly loved relative or friend, and that it is incumbent on their interlocutors to understand what it is.

Rapley (2004) contends that persons with intellectual disability are constructed in the way they are through their daily interactions with others. Much depends on how those others approach these interactions: whether they see themselves as interacting with persons who, because of their cognitive impairment, are incapable of engaging meaningfully in a conversation; or whether they see themselves as interacting with persons who, because of that very impairment and their life experiences, need to be understood on their own terms. Rapley's work provides the template for the latter type of interactions to take place in different contexts in life. The situations considered in this chapter show how important it is for such interactions to also be facilitated when a significant other of a person with intellectual disability is dying. They are, of course, also important when the person themself is nearing the end of their life (Read and Wiese 2022).

Rachel's struggle for words, Rosie's behaviour, and the words and actions of persons with intellectual disability whose grieving is described and analysed in Thorp et al.'s study, as well as in other accounts and research cited in this chapter, highlight the human connections that they forge with the people who play important roles in their lives. In mourning the loss of loved ones, persons with intellectual disability demonstrate the deep ties that they form with those around them. As Morgan (2022) says in the subtitle to the book about her son Pete – who, like Adam, had profound disabilities and died young – much can be said without any words being spoken.

Persons with intellectual disability mourn and are, in turn, themselves mourned when they die. The extent to which they mourn and eventually are mourned has nothing to do with their level of cognitive impairment. It has everything to do with how close and deeply ingrained the ties with the people around them are. Neither does it depend on how well they can communicate their grief, if at all, but on how deep in their heart their attachment with loved ones has been and continues to be after their loved ones are gone.

Note

1 Excerpt taken from page 49 of Nicki Thorp, Jacqui Stedmon and Helen Lloyd, 2018. 'I carry her in my heart': An exploration of the experience of bereavement for people with learning disability. *British Journal of Learning Disabilities*, 46(1), pp. 45–53. Used with permission from John Wiley & Sons.

15

LUCIEN GOES TO BED

> 'We are used to the occasional snap or nip from Lucien, but in recent weeks he has been biting as hard as he can. It's happening more often, to say nothing of the harm he can do with his hands. In years to come, his strength will only increase. A solution is called for and, in our view, he needs medication. It's an option we've discussed in the past; one you have refused to consider. But letting this go on until something even more serious occurs is a risk we cannot take. For the sake of his fellow residents,' she counted on her fingers. 'Our staff. And, of course, Lucien himself.'
>
> [. . .]
>
> 'No drugs,' Mum said, softly but stiffly. 'At home he was always a sweet, calm boy.'
>
> 'I am happy to believe that,' said the woman. 'But we have to base our conclusions on how he is functioning in this environment.'
>
> [. . .]
>
> He raised his hands. 'There's a reason we brought Lucien here. On days when I wasn't home, there were plenty of times when she couldn't handle him either.' Mum squeezed the blood from her knuckles.
>
> Robben (2021, pp. 163 and 164)[1]

These excerpts come from Jaap Robben's novel *Summer Brother* (2021). This contemporary story is narrated from the point of view of 13-year-old Brian, who lives in a trailer park with his father, who is divorced from his mother. He has a brother, Lucien, who is three years older and has intellectual and physical disabilities as well as communication difficulties. He has been institutionalised for many years. For one summer, Lucien goes to live with his brother and father while the place he lives in is being refurbished. It is the events of this summer that are recounted in the novel, with the arc of the narrative

DOI: 10.4324/9781003561644-15

interspersed with accounts of past events. The excerpts above, appearing more than halfway through the story, are from one such event that occurred when Brian was still living with both his parents; his brother had recently moved to the institution in which he is now living, and they were still visiting him regularly as a family. There is an incident that leads to the conversation presented above in which Lucien bites off Brian's earlobe. The staff's immediate reaction is to sedate Lucien since this is their standard procedure, as they explain to his mother, who protests that their policy constitutes abuse.

The novel starts with Brian and his father on their way to pay a rare visit to Lucien. The latter is mostly visited by his mother, whom the father does his best to avoid. The first thing we learn about Lucien is that he 'lives in a bed half an hour's drive from our caravan' (p. 14). This sentence immediately gives us the most important fact about Lucien's situation – that he 'lives in a bed'. It also gives us information about where Brian and his father live and where Lucien will be spending the summer.

Lucien's admission to the institution is a watershed in his life. Earlier in the novel, Brian recounts how, when Lucien moved there, he had the impression that his brother had been switched off and that he spent his time, from one Sunday visit to the next, asleep, dreaming of his family. At the time, Lucien was not yet being sedated. Brian's vision of his brother living in his bed turns out to be prescient. If he was confined to his bed up to the moment he tore his brother's earlobe, Lucien was to become even more bedbound thence. Being institutionalised means that Lucien goes to bed not in the common everyday sense in which one goes to bed for the night at home and gets out of it again after waking up in the morning. It is not even in the sense of going to bed when one is unwell and staying in it longer than usual, until one is well again. It is in the sense of Lucien going to bed in the institution and staying in it for most of the rest of his life; so much so that years later, at the point in time in which the opening scene of the novel is set, Brian describes him as living in his bed.

This description is a pithy indictment of all that is problematic about being in an institution. Lucien does not just live in an institution. He lives in a bed inside the institution. Describing Lucien as living in a bed focuses the reader's mind on just how restrictive institutional living is, even more so for those who, like Lucien, have high support needs. The guileless description by the adolescent Brian of his brother's living situation shows up the deleterious effects of institutional arrangements put in place by adults, supposedly to provide care for persons with disabilities who need types and degrees of support that cannot be provided directly by the family. It is a description that conjures up Erving Goffman's (1961) idea of the 'total institution', places providing congregate care whose residents are cut off from society for a long time, or even for the rest of their lives, and where every single aspect of their lives is completely controlled by those in authority.

The word 'institution' is not used at any time in the novel to describe the place where Lucien lives in his bed. Instead, it is referred to as 'the home'. This particular use of the word 'home' is, to all intents and purposes, a euphemistic substitute for institutional living. There is a world of difference between 'living at home' and 'living in the/a home', even if grammatically it is just a question of changing the preposition and inserting or removing the in/definite article. It is a world of difference because it is a completely different world that Lucien found himself in when he was taken away from his family home and placed in the residential home. Lucien's new world is very different, and in very many ways much better, than the one decried in Blatt and Kaplan's *Christmas in Purgatory* (1974), which first drew the outside world's attention to the horrors and blatant abuse of mass institutional living. Since then, much work has been done to close down large institutions and enable persons with intellectual and other types of disabilities to live in the community (Mansell and Ericsson 1996). The right to live in the community is also enshrined in the Convention on the Rights of Persons with Disabilities (2006), where 'Full and effective participation and inclusion in society' is one of the General Principles (Article 3(c)), Article 14 is dedicated to 'Liberty and security of the person' and Article 19 to 'Living independently and being included in the community'.

However, despite the fact that in many countries large-scale institutions have been closed, the process of deinstitutionalisation is incomplete (Committee on the Rights of Persons with Disabilities, 2015, 2017, 2022) and situations such as Lucien's still exist. Altermark (2017) argues that the current era should be seen as one of post-institutionalisation. The first part of this term acknowledges the positive changes that have been wrought, while the second part takes into account the way in which current residential services have characteristics that refer back to institutionalisation. In fact, Goffman's concept of total institutions is still used to critique many of the arrangements in residential services for persons with intellectual disability.

Niedbalski (2022) investigated the living conditions of persons with intellectual disability in Polish residential facilities. He discusses how, despite the changes put in place, it is still the staff who largely have control over the residents' lives, rather than the residents themselves. For example, one staff member commented on how residents were taken outside rather than always being on their ward, as used to happen in the past. But it is the staff who decide who goes out, when they go out and where they go. There is little scope for autonomy. Niedbalski speaks to a type of control in these facilities that 'totalizes and appropriates the subjectivity of an individual' (p. 81), negatively affecting the relationships between staff and residents and among the residents. Similar findings are presented by Guddingsmo (2022) and Svanelöv and Talman (2022) in their studies of Norwegian and Swedish residential homes, respectively. Furthermore, in research carried out in Spain,

Moyà-Köhler (2024) observes that the procedures used in places where persons with intellectual disability live have a deep impact on their ability to enjoy the right to independent living.

Niedbalski's (2022) study reports that one of the changes noted by a staff member interviewed was the switch from using physical restraints to medication. But this change is a sideways development rather than a step forward. The person is still subject to restraint and to having their life totally controlled by staff and, in turn, by those managing the institution. Perhaps Lucien's mother protests because she could see what would happen if her son was put on medication to control his behaviour. In fact, Lucien ended up in the same predicament as so many other inmates of long-term institutionalisation, however it manifests itself in different residential settings.

Lucien's mother's protests 'softly but stiffly', adverbs that evoke her tender regard for her son mixed with tension at the prospect of seeing him sedated. But, however justified she was in her resistance, she was outnumbered. Her protest that '[a]t home he was always a sweet, calm boy' is undermined by both the staff member in whose office they are and by the father. The latter's argument that the reason Lucien could not continue living at home was because of his behaviour might seem a valid one; but there is much more validity in the mother's protest than that argument, although it is obscured by the logic of the institution. The staff member tells Lucien's mother that she is 'happy to believe that' at home he was calm and sweet, with this expression coming across as a piece of verbal irony as it implies that in reality she did not believe her at all.

There is also much situational irony in this scene and its aftermath. The staff member seems to be taking Lucien's environment into account by pointing out that his behaviour at home and in the institution might be different, but it is the latter that needs to be considered because this is where he is. However, his presence in the institution is taken as inevitable. At no point is the suitability of its environment for Lucien questioned, except by his mother in her lone hapless protest. Furthermore, what is being considered is not the effect that this environment is having on Lucien, but the effect that he is having on the environment. The answer to why Lucien's behaviour has changed, from the occasional 'nip' to biting as hard as he can, is not looked for in his environment but in Lucien himself. The solution is not to change anything around Lucien that might be triggering his behaviour, but to control that behaviour. The sad irony is that what is proclaimed to be for Lucien's benefit is actually put in place for the benefit of others, and to his own detriment. What is even more ironic is that moving Lucien to the institution has not only not addressed his behavioural issues, but has also made them worse.

Lucien's situation has deteriorated; rather than the institution meeting his specific needs, he is made to fit into the rigours of the institution itself.

His personal welfare has been deprioritised through a decision presented in the guise of looking after him. This deprioritisation is epitomised in Brian's description of the staff member 'counting' the reasons for the need to place Lucien on medication, for pushing back against the resistance to taking this step shown by the mother until that point. The staff member mentions the other residents first, then the rest of the staff and, finally 'of course, Lucien himself'. The way Brian describes her as saying this – as counting the list of supposed beneficiaries of Lucien's medication on her fingers – implies that Lucien's own welfare comes third (and therefore also last) in the consideration.

Lucien's trauma of being separated from his family is also not considered. Harvey (2023) speaks of how that marginalisation creates trauma in the lives of persons with intellectual disability. This trauma is compounded when the person is separated from their family, like Lucien was; and it is in terms of response to trauma, including post-traumatic stress disorder (PTSD), that Harvey argues that behavioural issues need to be considered. In such circumstances, attack becomes the best form of defence for the person; but their behaviour continues to be seen as something to be managed, rather than a sign of psychological wounds that need to be healed. The staff member speaking to Lucien's mother only mentions the 'harm he can do with his hands' and how this can worsen as he grows bigger and stronger. There is no mention of the possibility that what Lucien does with his hands is his way of expressing his anguish, and that any worsening of his behaviour could reflect a worsening of his anguish and trauma.

Healing is possible, and the three key components for it to happen are identified by Harvey (2023): 'a sense of safety', 'connection to others' and 'a sense of power or agency over one's life' (p. 19). In the institution, Lucien was physically safe, but the medication he is given disconnects him from the people around him and from having any agency over his life. In such places, residents' lives are 'stolen' (Stolen Lives 2024). Lucien's mother feels this pain, and Brian picks up on her feeling it as he describes her squeezing the blood from her knuckles. But her voice and Lucien's, and their pain, are not acknowledged.

Having been taken away from his familial network, Lucien's distress is compounded by not allowing him to develop connections and relations with the other residents and the staff of his new home. This happens because the place where he is now living is not a real home, but an institution. Had it been a real home, those managing it would have considered how, taken away from his most intimate network, Lucien is traumatised. He is no longer in an environment where he is surrounded by people who understand him because they have grown accustomed to his idiosyncratic way of communicating, like he was at home. He is now *in the* home and no longer *at* home. In the home, Lucien's 'Mah-mah-mmah!' (Robben 2021, p. 19) and other vocalisations are meaningless and ignored, until he has to resort to hitting out at others to signal his distress. At home, these vocalisations are understood as laden with meaning, expressing needs that had to be met – like 'if there was food on the table and he couldn't reach' (p. 19), as Brian tells us early in the novel. Lucien's physical attack is not just a means of psycho-emotional defence but a counter-attack against the psycho-emotional violence wrought on him when he was no longer at home but in the home, when he was longer primarily a brother and son but another resident whose problematic behaviour needed to be administered away.

The non-linear structure of Brian's narrative of the summer that Lucien spent with him and his father in their caravan highlights the contrast between how Lucien ended up once he was in the residential home and what he was like at home, a state which is briefly rediscovered when he spends the summer with his brother. We first meet Lucien after he permanently goes to bed in the home. We then see him gradually coming out of his torpor once he goes to his father and brother's home; and we also see him as he was earlier, when he was still at home with the whole family. The home he has for that summer is a ramshackle caravan in which his specialised hospital bed does not fit and he has to sleep outside. He cannot even be said to be living in the caravan, but beside it. The father is only after the money he would be paid for putting his son up for the summer. He makes sure that no one from the home actually sees where Lucien is living. Had they done so they would have decried the completely inappropriate physical environment. Had they kept watch on what was going on they would have been appalled at how Lucien's care is left in the hands of his younger brother, with the father all but abrogating responsibility for it. On paper, this environment is no match for the properly equipped one provided in the home. But, on an interpersonal level, the environment in the home is no match for the enriching one provided in this seemingly inadequate home.

Around one-fifth into the novel, Brian strikes up a conversation with Thibault, the physiotherapist working in the home where Lucien has been placed, who explains to Brian that his brother could walk if only he was supported to get the physical exercise he needed. In the home, not only is Lucien not shown the kind of affection he had within the family, but he does not even get adequate stimulation. At the summer home, beside the caravan, he gets the affection and stimulation he needs from Brian, who uses his brotherly instincts to figure out not just how to take care of Lucien but how to connect with him at the deepest level.

At the end of the novel, Lucien is back in the home, 'folded up and tucked away, somewhere deep inside himself' (p. 266). Brian resolves to take Lucien to live with him when he is older and has his own home. Perhaps he will manage to do that, following the footsteps of real-life persons with intellectual disability, such as Judith Scott and Jill Kohfield, who were taken out of institutions by family members and thrived (see Scott n.d. and Strauss 2015).

Meanwhile, Lucien remains in the home, in bed and cut off from everyone and everything meaningful in his life.

Note

1 Excerpts taken from pp. 163 and 164 of *Summer Brother* by Jaap Robben, translated by David Doherty. Used with permission of the publisher, World Editions. Copyright © 2021, World Editions.

16

PERSONS WITH INTELLECTUAL DISABILITY, KITH AND KIN

Leap-year day, 29 February, that rarest of calendar days, is Rare Disease Day (observed on the 28th in non-leap years) (Rare Disease Day 2024). On 29 February 2024, Eva Kittay marked it with a Facebook post celebrating the life of her daughter Sesha, whose condition (PURA syndrome) is very rare. The condition arises from a variant of just one gene which has a significant impact on many areas of development and functioning. However, what Kittay focuses on in this post are the characteristics that make Sesha who she is in all her magnificence. The following are excerpts from that post:

> Sesha is now 54 years old, and little could we have imagined then, the joy she would bring into our lives and the magnificent person she has developed into. Yes, all the difficulties that were prognosticated [. . .] are still with her. [. . .] But the long list of conditions she has does not sum up who she is [. . .] She has taught me that so many philosophical dogmas I had taken for granted were missing important aspects of our lives. She has inspired me to rethink and write about these matters. She has taught me how to listen – really listen – to music. And to understand how very little we know of what happens in the minds of those labeled intellectually disabled. [. . .] I venture she has found ways to deal with pain, frustration, sadness, and other difficulties in ways most of us have not. Depriving ourselves of knowledge of people such as my daughter is depriving ourselves of knowledge of who and what we are as human beings. Sesha is a great gift to me and to all who know her. Her presence in this troubled world makes the world a more livable place.[1]

DOI: 10.4324/9781003561644-16

This penned portrait of Sesha is of a person who has meaningful reciprocal relations with people who know her; who has not only found her own way of enjoying life but who also brings joy to others. Kittay's post goes even further than that by observing how – to use the wording from her book's title (Kittay 2019b) – what she has learnt from her daughter can tell us much not only about persons with intellectual disability but also about human beings more generally.

Kittay's Facebook post is therefore a fitting way to start this concluding chapter. Having had a brief but intense glimpse into the lives of Josephine, Noli, Marc's students, Eve, Giovanni Mazzariol, Lauren Potter, the Focus Group E interviewee, Participant 13's service-users, Noelle, Leon, Shea MacDonough, Rachel, and Brian and his brother Lucien, we can appreciate the impact that reciprocal relationships – or their absence – can have on the lives of persons with intellectual disability.

We can also see how the impact affects much more than what each person is able to do or not in and with their lives. It also affects their very selves and their perspectives on life, as well as the effect they have on others and the perspectives the latter have of them.

The analyses in the preceding chapters bring out the interconnections of the lives of persons with intellectual disability – especially those with whom they form close and lasting ties, but also with those who they encounter more casually or transiently and through structural arrangements and social practices. Whether the impact of these interconnections is affirmative or deleterious depends heavily on the mindset of those who interact with them, directly or indirectly. The analyses address this book's main theme, as stated in Chapter 1 – the interconnectedness of human relations, the emergence of the sense of self from both internal factors and from these relations, and their embedding in the human heart.

A synthesis of the preceding chapters shows the common enabling and disabling factors experienced by the persons with intellectual disability who featured in them. There are many commonalities that can be considered, and this final chapter focuses on those which are relevant to the theme of the book. The next section discusses how the lives of the persons with intellectual disability featured are intertwined and connected with those of others. The focus then turns to the implications of seeing these persons with intellectual disabilities as rightsholders. The scenes analysed in the preceding chapters are then discussed with reference to the concepts from Bruner's and Ricoeur's work presented in Chapter 1, with the discussion referring back to this book's title. The applicability of critical phenomenology to the book's main theme is considered next. The chapter closes with an accessible summary of the main points of the book.

Intertwining and connecting

The 14 excerpts discussed in the preceding chapters are necessarily interconnected with events that preceded and, in some cases, followed the scenes they present, events which are brought into the discussion. Understanding the lived experience of persons with intellectual disability entails looking at their past and current experiences, how they connect with each other. Comparing and contrasting the different situations lends itself to more in-depth understanding. The focus here is on what the excerpts, and the linked events, reflect about how persons with intellectual disability relate to others and how others relate to them. This element of relationality is significant regardless of whether these others are family members, friends, those who are learning or working alongside them or those paid to play a direct role in their lives – educators, employers, job coaches, support workers, classmates, workmates and fellow performers. It is also a significant element to consider for those whose relationship with the person with intellectual disability is regular but indirect, such as customers, ancillary staff in institutions and family acquaintances. And it is significant for those whose encounters with persons with intellectual disability are more transient or distant – interviewers, members of an audience, filmmakers and photographers and members of decision-making bodies.

These aspects of relationality are significant for anyone, with or without an intellectual disability. However, the support needs of many persons with intellectual disability mean that 'many have an external locus of control' (O'Brien and Duffy 2022, p. 49). Consequently, their dependence on others in many aspects of their daily lives makes the dispositions of other persons towards them highly impactful. These dispositions impinge on how others behave with persons with intellectual disability, what decisions they make and actions they take in their regard and how they speak to them. These dispositions, in turn, are impacted by preconceived ideas about intellectual disability (which can be affirmatory or harmful) and by laws, policies, institutional arrangements and structural practices.

For the persons with intellectual disability who feature in the 14 extracts, their relationships with others are characterised by a mixture of affirmative, neutral and negative encounters. In the case of the extracts that give us a glimpse into family life, we see wholesome relationships being developed. Eve's photo shows her ensconced in the nurturing safety of her family. Leon needs his mother when school becomes overwhelming. Rachel mourns her grandfather and Shea is motivated to reclaim her vote to support her cousin's gay marriage. Josephine's narrative is interspersed with her mother's, evincing the care and support the latter provides. Giovanni and Lucien too receive care and support from their families. Unfortunately, not all families of persons with intellectual disability are as caring and supportive, and some are outright abusive (Keeley et al. 2023). But, for these seven persons, the family home is a place where they are accepted and nurtured. It is in their encounters with some others outside the home that trouble arises.

Josephine's experience in mainstream schools has been a mixture of the good and the bad. The scene in the gym appears as mundane as that of the caretaker in Leon's school inviting the boy to help carry boxes and of Giacomo and Giovanni going together the carnival in their hometown together. It is the very ordinariness of these three encounters that makes them extraordinary. In Josephine's case, her classmates' laughter and the educators' problematic solution are painful reminders that her attending a mainstream school does not mean she is fully accepted. She has to conform to preset standards. For Leon, the caretaker's simple invitation unwittingly provides a lesson to his educators about the need to connect with him on his own terms. In Giovanni's case, his excitement of going to the carnival with his brother is superseded, unbeknown to him at the time, by Giacomo's life-defining decision to proclaim his status as Giovanni's brother to the world, thus confronting the prejudice it holds against persons with intellectual disability.

Eve's family too encounter this prejudice in the sympathy card sent to her father. Prejudice is experienced in a different manner by Shea, who is assumed not to have the capacity to vote by decision-makers who never met her but who have enough strongly ingrained misconceptions to give them the false confidence of thinking they can sit in judgement over the supposed incapacities of persons with intellectual disability. Tragically, these misconceptions exist even within services that are supposed to nurture these persons, like the home Lucien ends up in.

Rachel's close family ties emerge through her grief for her grandfather. His loss accentuates her close ties with him. Loss also features in situations outside the family home. Noelle's poem foregrounds the contrast between having and not having friends, and how this impacts how she feels about herself. For Marc's students, the tight control he maintains over them does not just translate into a lost opportunity to develop practical self-determination skills; it is also a reinforcement of their sense of haplessness and inability to make decisions for themselves. Marc's decision is as unappealable as the bartender's not to serve alcohol to Focus Group Participant E. These are decisions which are based entirely on a deficit model of intellectual disability, with no consideration of how a supportive disposition enables persons with intellectual disability to develop self-determination skills and breaks the vicious cycle of lack of opportunities abetting lack of development, and vice versa.

In other extracts, we witness what can happen when this cycle is broken or avoided altogether. The service-users who Research Participant 13 works with have much more profound cognitive impairments than Focus Group Participant E. The latter could express his frustration verbally and directly to the researchers. The former's wishes and preferences need to be interpreted. P13 works on the supposition that there are wishes and preferences to be interpreted, and sets forth to find a way to do that. The contrast between the disposition of the bartender and P13 highlights how many obstacles encountered by persons with intellectual disability arise not from their impairments but from other people's presumptions about their capacity or lack thereof.

When these attitudes are oriented towards supporting persons with intellectual disability to fulfil their potential, towards affirming their personhood as fellow human beings, further possibilities open up. The support for Noli to enter the labour market has enabled her to earn money and work towards her dream of living independently and to provide a necessary service to the market stall owner. As her work role evolved, further possibilities presented themselves – for example, her helping some customers with carrying their shopping. Likewise, Lauren's successful acting career was a launchpad for her to be more actively involved in the film industry and to use her fame to campaign for disability rights. In Brian's case, his experience of co-producing and staging plays enabled him to take a sophisticated dig at those who argue that he could not possibly have contributed to the development of the play he was acting in.

Thus, it can be seen how important it is to attend to the nature of the connections that persons with intellectual disability have with others, and to ensure that the way they intertwine with each other engenders growth and further possibilities while consciously avoiding the creation of situations that suffocate this development. The effect of such suffocation can be seen at its worst in Lucien's plight. Avoiding it is also, but not only, a question of rights.

Rights, but not only rights

The preceding chapters have all referred to the Convention on the Rights of Persons with Disabilities (2006) (CRPD). The social dimension to disability, heralded by the social model (Oliver 1990), introduced obligations towards persons with disabilities that go beyond the provision of medical care, rehabilitation and welfare. The social model provokes change in the physical environment, in structural and institutional arrangements and practices, and in attitudes. Affirming the rights of persons with disability and inscribing them into legislation further raises the character of the changes from favours and acts of charity to formal obligations and respect of rights.

Anti-discrimination disability legislation, starting with the Americans with Disability Act in 1990 and culminating in the CRPD 26 years later, is a product of the paradigmatic change in attitudes instilled by the disability movement. The change also encompasses how persons with disability look at themselves as they realise that their situation is not an inevitable consequence of having an impairment. Much more needs to be done for them to enjoy the human rights and fundamental freedoms enshrined in the 1948 Universal Declaration of Human Rights. In her analysis of the situation of persons with disability in France, Anne Revillard (2023) shows that disability rights legislation and policy are not enough to combat all the discrimination, unfair treatment and obstacles that they experience. However, they do go a long way towards redressing disability-related injustices. Additionally, as Revillard argues, disability rights legislation affects the very identity of persons with disability. Generally speaking, the younger disabled participants in her research were more likely to interpret their difficulties as disregard of their rights and to fight for those rights than the older participants, who tended to be grateful for any help and good fortune that came their way.

Consequently, considering the rights of persons with intellectual disability is relevant to the discussion of their lived experience. Rights legislation leads to changes from the macro to the micro level; from policies, services and measures being put in place to ensure that the rights inscribed by law are realized to changes in one-to-one interactions when persons with intellectual disability are seen as rightsholders. Furthermore, being rightsholders affords persons with intellectual disability the possibility of surer ground on which to make certain claims. For example, legislation affirming the right to work (also inscribed in CRPD Article 27, 'Work and employment') for persons with disability needs to be made a reality through, among others, job carving and providing job coaches for persons with intellectual disability. This is how Noli secured her job at the fruit and vegetable stall in the market.

Josephine's sockless feet remind us that having arrangements in place for implementing rights legislation is not enough to ensure that rights are realised. Like all other rights, the right to inclusive education (CRPD Article 24, 'Education') needs to be worked at constantly, with adaptations being made according to the needs of each student. The lesson that the caretaker in Leon's school inadvertently gives his educators is a good example of this need. Awareness of how rights connect with each other is also necessary. The differential treatment between Marc's students, who have intellectual disability, and the other students from the same school on the trip to Paris, does not only highlight the inferior status of the former. It is also an instance of a missed opportunity afforded by the trip for the students with intellectual disability to be supported to develop self-determination skills for an adulthood in which they can 'participate effectively in a free society' (CRPD Article 24.1(c)). But if they continue to be treated like children, the potential of Marc's students as adults cannot emerge; neither are they likely to manage to assert other rights associated with adult life.

The way that recognising and nurturing the potential of persons with intellectual disability engenders the realisation of other rights can be seen in the achievements of Noli, Brian and Lauren. Noli's aim of working to earn money to be able to live independently also taps into Article 19 (Living independently and being included in the community). For Brian and Lauren, their stage and film work is also connected with Article 30 (Participation in cultural life, recreation, leisure and sport). Their presence on stage and screen showcases the status that should be afforded to all persons with intellectual disability, regardless of the personae they are acting out.

Achievements in one area, however, do not necessarily translate into the recognition of all rights for a person with intellectual disability. Like Lauren, Shea is a disability rights activist, and yet had to fight to reclaim her right to vote and participate in political processes, as affirmed in CRPD Article 29 (Participation in political and public life). Shea's challenge to the Australian Electoral Commission's (AEC) decision also taps into CRPD Article 12 (Equal recognition before the law), which asserts the right to the recognition of legal capacity for all persons with disability, regardless of their mental capacity, and therefore of being able to take decisions about their own lives, with support as and when necessary. Once again, Marc's students' predicament is relevant here as an example of how persons with intellectual disability can be denied a say even in ordinary decisions.

These students' frustration is echoed by Focus Group Participant E, who was denied being served the drink they chose without any explanation or possibility of appeal. Both situations show how the realisation of rights depends heavily on personal interactions with each and every individual with intellectual disability. Starting from a premise of incapacity forecloses opportunities for growth. Had Focus Group Participant E been given a valid explanation as to why they could not be served the drink they wanted, there would at least have been an acknowledgement of their capacity to understand why certain decisions are made. But, as things stand, we do not even know whether the decision was the right one. What is purportedly done in the best interests of the person with intellectual disability is detrimental.

In contrast, we have P13 and other support workers who take decisions on behalf of service-users with severe and multiple impairments who cannot express themselves verbally about the use of their leisure time on the premise that they too can enjoy a good life. What these workers do may not fit within 'the best interpretation of will and preferences' approach advocated by the Committee on the Rights of Persons with Disabilities (2014) in General Comment No. 1 on Article 12 when a person's will and preferences cannot be easily determined. Whether they could do more to gauge the service-users' will and preferences is an important question. But a more relevant point here is that, by choosing the leisure activities that they themselves enjoy, these support workers place the service-users on the same footing as themselves and seek to engage in equitable relationships with them.

Having disability rights legislation and the structural arrangements to implement it are important because they facilitate the provision of necessary support and adjustments by making them obligatory; because they can give persons with intellectual disability the confidence and assertiveness to protest when they are denied what is theirs by right; and because they enable those who live, work or otherwise relate to persons with intellectual disability to recognise their human dignity in their interactions.

But rights are not enough. They are a means to an end, not an end in themselves. They are a means to creating environments in which Noelle need never feel less than whole because she is without her friends, and in which Rachel's grief at the loss of her grandfather is fully acknowledged and allowed to be articulated. Rights can only play an indirect (though still important) role in these scenarios. After all, neither friendship nor grieving is inscribed as a right in any piece of legislation. They play a more direct role for Eve – sustaining her right to life (CRPD Article 10) – and fail to do so for Lucien, whose right to live independently and be included in the community (Article 19) is completely quashed by the institution he is in. But even here, what is affirmative in Eve's situation and harmful in Lucien's goes beyond their rights. It is about relationships that recognise their humanity, interacting with them as fellow human beings while attending to their impairment-related needs. This is what Eve's photograph tells us about what is going well in her life. This is what Lucien's story tells us about all the things that have gone horribly wrong in his, except for that one summer he spent with his brother.

Without informal recognition of the humanity of persons with intellectual disability, regardless of how severe and complex their impairments might be, formally recognised rights remain abstract notions. What non-disabled people do and say in their interactions with these persons has a profound effect on their lives, on the conceptual and practical levels. The nurturing environment that Sesha Kittay has inhabited from her infancy is another example of the profound effect of affirmative relationships. Her mother's Facebook post celebrates Sesha's life to date. As Eva Kittay argues here and elsewhere (including 2019a, 2019b), knowing Sesha is not just knowing a human being, but also knowing more about human being.

Oneself in kith, kin and others

One of the most important things that we learn about the persons with intellectual disability we have encountered in this book is how deeply intertwined their lives are with those of other people, and how many connections impinge on their lives. Jerome Bruner's concept of the distributed self and Paul Ricoeur's argument about the fundamental role played by others in the development of one's *ipse*-identity can be clearly discerned in the experiences discussed. These factors can be also perceived in the way that the past affects the present; in interactions with people who are close to the person with intellectual disability and those whose contact is infrequent or indirect; in the immediate environment and the service provision and legislative landscape; and in social, cultural, political and economic factors.

Bruner's and Ricoeur's work on how the human self develops applies to persons with and without intellectual disability simply because they are all human. But the dependence of those with intellectual disability on others, to a greater degree than most other persons, makes consideration of these various connections all the more important. When Giovanni's parents convinced him not to wake his brother up, they were reacting to his past behaviour patterns. They were aware of how he would not be able to contain his excitement, and knew what would work to convince him to do that. When Giacomo agreed to go out with Giovanni in public – on the day '[a] lot of people, practically all of Castelfranco' (Mazzariol 2020, p. 132) were out – he was reacting to a panoply of factors: affirming his blood ties with his younger brother; working on resolving his remorse at not having acknowledged him as his brother even when he needed to be saved from bullies; and ditching the sociocultural disablist norms that had motivated his behaviour in the first place. Giacomo's narrative is also a coming-of-age narrative, and his public affirmation of himself as Giovanni's brother is a sign of his leaving adolescent immaturity behind him.

Thus, there is a continuous back-and-forth movement from individuals with intellectual disability to others, interspersed by various factors within an intricate web of direct and indirect, long-lasting and transient interactions. How people behave with persons with intellectual disability and what they say to or about them matters deeply. It is in one-to-one interactions that the impact of different factors is felt and can be perceived. These factors align well for Noli but badly for Marc's students. It is not a coincidence that Noli speaks about both her support needs and her future plans with equal confidence and assertiveness, while Marc's students can only helplessly complain to researcher Godefroy Lansade about their predicament. Here, we can see Ricoeur's *ipse*- and *idem*-identities at work. Noli and the students remain the same persons, with the same *idem*-identity; but Noli's sense of self is bolstered through the way she is supported, how she is spoken about and how her work is validated. Marc's students' sense of self is wounded. When Lansade asks Noa why he hadn't protested about his teacher's tight control over his money, the student replied that he wouldn't have been able to express himself. The presumption by others of his incompetence reaches into Noa's own assumptions about his lack ability to articulate his thoughts and feelings.

There is enough evidence in the brief exchange between Noa and Lansade to show how mistaken this assumption is. Noa is aware of the unequal treatment meted out to him and his mates in the ULIS inclusive education programme and of the possibility of protesting against it. But he is also aware of how futile this would be because he cannot do it effectively. Like Rachel,

Noa does not quite know how to verbalise his thoughts and feelings. Unlike her, he does not have an interlocutor who probes and prods to enable him to express himself. The same pattern can be seen in the complaint by Focus Group Participant E about the barman's peremptory dismissal of their order at the bar.

For Noa and his ULIS mates, the injurious exchange happens in their adolescence, at a time when their peers are preparing themselves for adulthood. As discussed in Chapter 1, to be a human adult is most often taken to mean to be able to assume sole responsibility for oneself and one's actions, to be a rational person and to be autonomous of others in day-to-day decisions and actions. The daily support needs of persons with intellectual disability challenge these expectations. Unfortunately, there has long been a denial of these persons' status as adults, and even as humans (Carlson 2023), instead of revising the concept of adulthood and personhood in the first place. There are no indications that Bruner's and Ricoeur's work was developed with those who have cognitive impairment specifically in mind. The fact that it is in any case so relevant is highly significant. It shows how well this work speaks to what it is to be human because it can be applied to interactions with all humans, no matter what their cognitive capacity.

Ricoeur does analyse the type of relationships where the other's impact on one's self is damaging. As seen in Chapter 1, he recognises the unidirectional nature of this impact. This 'power-over', as Ricoeur terms it, can lead to violence. It has often done so for people with intellectual disability. An example of the violence perpetrated on them is not considering them as priorities for treatment in the ravages of the Covid-19 pandemic (Carlson 2023).

The violence can be more mundane and can occur in seemingly harmless, even well-intentioned, interactions. One example is Josephine being told to cover up her toes, with the school not realising the injury committed to the child's sense of self. Applying the Golden Rule, we can ask: how would the educators feel if they were told to cover up a part of their body that drew laughter from others, as happened to Josephine? This question can be extended to other scenes. How would the AEC members feel if their right to vote was denied them because of preconceived ideas about their ability to understand what the vote is, as happened to Shea? How would the audience member in Back to Back Theatre's performance feel if he was publicly and loudly told that he could not possibly be able to do something that he was doing, as happened to Brian and his fellow performers? How would the staff in Lucien's home (which is a home but not home) feel if they were left in bed most of the day on heavy medication, without any stimulation, without being able to express themselves and be understood, and only seeing family at most once a week?

These questions affirm the humanity of Josephine, Shea, Brian, Lucien and all persons with intellectual disability. It is through attending to these needs that their humanity can be affirmed, their selfhood sustained and their personhood flourish. It is this affirmative approach that we see unfolding in the two exchanges between David and Brian in the Back to Back Theatre scenes. What, in the second excerpt, appears to be David undoing the encouragement he gives Brian and the other performers in the first excerpt is actually providing support through bounded freedom. First, David boosts Brian's confidence by confirming his authorship of 'the springboard' and that of the other performers by inviting them 'to do the dive' and make the swim their own. Then he curbs Brian's ideas and talks of a freedom which is fixed. What these two scenes in the play within the play do is provide a great example of a framework in which the self of the person with intellectual disability and that of the non-disabled other can meet in a context of 'power-in-common', to use Ricoeur's term. The reciprocity may seem to be lopsided; but we must remember that, in acting out the second scene, Brian is in on the jest of exercising his agency as an actor who is pretending to be controlled by another. These observations also remind us of Ricoeur's observation that, even with the Golden Rule, there is an implied asymmetry, with one person doing the action and the other being acted upon.

This power-in-common offers many possibilities for the self to bloom in its relations with the other through attending to impairment-related needs and the provision of support. We can even see this power-in-common in the way P13 approaches their work with service-users with severe cognitive and additional impairments. The questions they ask themselves are the Golden Rule in action – what would they want to do if they were in the service-users' place? Since they cannot obtain a direct answer, they put the service-users in their own shoes and enable them to experience the type of leisure activities that they themselves enjoy. These service-users are thus also supported to exercise some agency in their lives. This brings us to the third type of power considered by Ricoeur, the power-to-act. When the support provided and the interactions it entails are oriented towards affirming the selfhood of the person with intellectual disability, all those involved in the interaction can exercise their agency with and through each other.

For these support-providing interactions to be possible, both the immediate and the wider context need to be conducive to the building of wholesome relationships. For Leon, living in a country that has adopted an inclusive education policy and which has provided resources to implement, it was essential for him to attend a mainstream school, even if with difficulties. But, in the midst of the storm he was creating as he was venting his frustration by kicking the cardboard boxes, it was the immediate context that needed to change. All it took was a simple invitation through which the caretaker connected with Leon as one human being to another.

This serene, wholesome context also comes across in Eve's photograph. Her family are providing her with the nurturing support that she needs to flourish as a person with Down syndrome, with the most important thing about her being that she is a human being. But Down syndrome is also tough, and Eve also needs support.

What we see in these 14 scenes is how one-to-one encounters, the here and now, bring to bear on each situation dispositions that are already there and create experiences that open up to or close off different kinds of present and future possibilities. These encounters take place in contexts that are partly determined by law- and decision-makers who put in place the formal structures for the rights of persons with intellectual disability, among others, to be realized. Service-providing organisations play an equally significant role. The parents' accounts presented in Lacherelle's (2023) book are testimony to its subtitle: *Grandir ensemble*, 'Growing up together'. The family of the person with intellectual disability grows with the person, and the services provided by professionals become an integral part of this process.

The most important factors remain the way in which a person with intellectual disability can exercise agency and how this agency is supported (or undermined) by what the one interacting with a person with intellectual disability says and does, and how the latter is provided with any support they need. These two elements are intertwined and impinge on each other. This is why, when reflecting on the lived experience of persons with intellectual disability, it is vital to consider the role of kith and kin.

The *Oxford English Dictionary* shows that 'kith and kin', dating from at least the fourteenth century, originally referred to compatriots and relatives. While 'kin' has retained its meaning, 'kith' later came to refer to acquaintances and friends. The dictionary notes that it is 'in modern use often taken merely as a pleonastic phrase for Kinsfolk, relatives, family connections'. In her discussion of the place of persons with intellectual disability in a rural community, Ellis (2017) makes a strong argument for reclaiming the older meaning of 'kith' to refer to those with whom one has close ties, the ones who help create a sense of belonging in their own community for persons with intellectual disability.

Here, too, 'kith' is being used in the sense of those the person knows and who know the person outside the family. Through this term, we can consider how relationships work for persons with intellectual disability. When they are young, they are likely to have professionals involved in their lives that other children do not have, such as Leon having a learning support educator in class and an inclusion coordinator also involved in his education. As adults, they may also have close contact with people who work with them specifically because they have an intellectual disability, such as Noli's job coach. In addition, for those who live in supported housing, like P13's service-users, they come into close contact with workers in their own home. Persons with intellectual disability are therefore likely to have relationships that are not common for the rest of the population. Additionally, they can form friend-like attachments with the people they are most often in contact with. This was discussed in the analysis of Noelle's poem and is also taken up by Ellis (2017), who argues that what she calls 'kithship' is a useful term to describe close relationships that persons with intellectual disability enjoy in their communities. Therefore, following Ellis's call, 'kith' here is being 'exhume[d]' (p. 228) to refer to friends, acquaintances and those who the person with intellectual disability forms close connections with.

The role of kith and kin is also taken to go much deeper than fostering a sense of belonging in one's own community, important as this is. Following Ricoeur, we need to consider what others bring to relationships with persons with intellectual disability and what they bring to their relationship with others. Talk of 'persons with intellectual disability' and 'others' is not meant to create two distinct and opposing groups. After all, everyone is other because everyone is unique. But there are enough commonalities to make it useful to think of the general characteristics of particular groups of people while steering away from essentialism. However, such distinctions are only useful insofar as they can help identify what works for them and what doesn't.

Understanding one's relationship with persons with intellectual disability as kith, regardless of the role one plays in their lives, can enable us to get the balance right: the balance between respecting their inherent equality with other human beings and respecting the particular support needs that having a cognitive impairment often entails; and the balance between recognising them as agents in their own lives and recognising the degree to which they depend on others to exercise it. This 'kithship' (to use Ellis's term) also enables us to understand the reciprocity of this relationship and how, as Kittay states in her Facebook post, getting to know a person with intellectual disability also tells us much about 'who and what we are as human beings'. The most significant thing it tells us is that, as Ricoeur states, '[t]he *autonomy* of the self will appear to be tightly bound up with *solicitude* for one's neighbor and with *justice* for each individual' (1992, p. 18, emphasis in the original).

A critical perspective of the lived experience

The close ties we have with each other are reflected in the way we affect each other's very self. Furthermore, the relationships that emanate from these ties are played out in specific historic and sociocultural contexts. Consequently, an examination of any lived experience needs to consider interpersonal connections and wider factors. The effect that all these factors have on one's selfhood has been shown repeatedly in the analyses and discussions presented in this book.

Using critical phenomenology as part of my conceptual framework meant that the analyses considered personal as well as social factors as integral parts of the lived experience. Using Max Van Manen's approach, I have focused on specific instances in the lives of persons with intellectual disability. Combining these two elements meant being able to zoom in on the intricacies of each scene while widening the focus to examine how it is connected to other events and to the broader context in which it happens. This bidirectional process of analysis has been very revealing. Van Manen's appeal to engage in 'musing, reflective questioning, and being obsessed' (2016b, p. 26) has proven to be a very fruitful way of conducting phenomenological inquiry. As I hope to have shown in here and in the preceding chapters, there are multiple layers of meaning to be discovered and revealed through an iterative process of reflecting on the microscopic details of an excerpt, and simultaneously considering other events that happened in the life of the protagonist of any given scene and the sociocultural context in which they occurred. Additionally, as Van Manen argues, the variety of excerpts used shows how lived experience can be analysed through different types of text, including research data, narratives, playscripts, photographs, poems, interviews and letters.

As a penultimate step for this book, I return to the three questions set out in Chapter 1 to discuss how they were addressed through this methodology. The first question asked: Whose perspective(s) should be used to reach an understanding of the lived experience of persons with intellectual disability? The most obvious answer is the perspective of the person(s) with intellectual disability themselves. But it also goes beyond that. The intertwining of their lives with that of others, especially of their kin and kith, means that other persons' perspectives are also crucial. Time and again we have seen how each one-to-one interaction with a person with intellectual disability is informed by pre-established ideas (whether affirmatory or otherwise) and how they, in turn, impact on that person's selfhood.

The second question asked: When we can know that we have reached an adequate understanding of the lived experience of persons with intellectual disability? There is probably no point at which we can say we have arrived. One reason is that, for any scene under analysis, there are myriad factors to consider and details can be broken down into smaller and smaller details. Another reason is that one's lived experience is dynamic. Given that phenomenological inquiry can only happen adequately after the fact, once the analysis starts the person will have moved on to other experiences that also merit analysis.

The final question referred to what the answers to these questions can tell us about persons with intellectual disability as fellow human beings and, therefore, about humanity itself. The ways in which Bruner's concept of the distributed self and Ricoeur's relational self show how the human self works are as applicable to persons with intellectual disability as they are to humanity in general. The deep connections that persons with intellectual disability experience with others, especially those who live and work closely with them, draw our attention to how we are all, in fact, closely interconnected, and that we would not be who we are without the people we consider to be our kith and kin. At the same time, we must remain attentive to the greater degree of dependency on others that many persons with intellectual disability experience throughout their lives to help ensure they are provided with the support they need while being able to live life 'on an equal basis with others', as the CRPD decrees.

One dimension of the support needs of persons with intellectual disability is access to information. I am keenly aware of the fact that the way that this book is written makes it difficult for many persons with intellectual disability to easily understand. As a way of compensating for that, however inadequately, the final section of the book comprises a list of main points written in accessible language.

Accessible summary of the main points

- This book presents scenes from the lives of some persons with intellectual disability so that we can better understand their experiences.
- Persons with intellectual disability are not always accepted by others. When Josephine was in primary school, her classmates laughed when she took her socks off in the gym because her feet looked different from theirs.
- Persons with intellectual disability are not always given the chance to learn how to be independent. When Marc, who is a teacher, took a group of young persons with intellectual disability on a school trip to Paris, he did not allow them to spend any money in the way they wished.
- Decisions can be made without them being explained to persons with intellectual disability. When a person with intellectual disability ordered a drink at a bar, they were told they couldn't be served alcohol, with no explanation.
- Decisions can also be made without considering the abilities of a person with intellectual disability. When Shea applied to get her vote back, it was assumed that she couldn't vote. She had to make a complaint to enable her to vote.
- But there are also many persons with intellectual disability who receive the support they need. Thanks to this support, Noli was able to find a job in the market and provide a valuable service.
- Being able to do one thing can lead to other achievements. Lauren Potter has used her success as an actress to become a film producer and an advocate for persons with Down syndrome.
- For persons with intellectual disability to build on their achievements, it is important that they receive the support they need. Brian can develop scripts and act in plays through guidance from others.
- It is also very important for persons with intellectual disability to be accepted as they are. Giovanni's brother Giacomo found it difficult to

admit he had a brother with Down syndrome when he was growing up. But he finally managed to overcome this difficulty and took Giovanni to the local carnival.

- When a person with intellectual disability cannot communicate verbally, it is important to work with them to see what they enjoy doing. Some support workers provide different leisure opportunities to see which ones are most enjoyable for the persons with severe intellectual and multiple impairments they work with.
- When a person has difficulty communicating verbally, they can become very frustrated and their behaviour can become challenging. This is what happened to Leon at school. The caretaker calmed him down by asking him to help carry boxes, showing that Leon was accepted.
- It is important to appreciate the close ties that persons with intellectual disability have with their families. Rachel was very sad when her grandfather died, but she needed support to be able to express her emotions.
- Friendships are also very important for persons with intellectual disability. In her poem, Noelle tells us that she does not feel whole without her friends.
- When persons with intellectual disability are not supported, their lives become sad and empty. This happens to Lucien when he goes into a home where he is kept in bed and given a lot of drugs to keep him calm.
- When persons with intellectual disability grow up in a home where there is love and support, they flourish. We see a photo of Eve with her family who protect her as she is growing up with Down syndrome and love her for who she is.
- To get to know a person with intellectual disability we should listen to what they and the people closest to them have to say about their lives. What Eva Kittay tells us about her daughter Sesha helps us appreciate her and her life.
- Persons with intellectual disability are just like other human beings, even though they have more support needs. Learning about their lives enables us to understand how we can support them and how all human beings need to support each other.
- What matters most is that persons with and without intellectual disability relate to each other as equals.

Note

1 Excerpt taken from a Facebook post by Eva Kittay on 29 February 2024. Used with permission from the author.

ACKNOWLEDGEMENTS

Various people have had an impact, directly or indirectly, on my work on this book. My first thanks go to all those who produced the material from which I took the excerpts that I discuss in each chapter. They shed light on the lived experience of persons with intellectual disability and those closest to them – through research, autobiographies, playscripts, novels, poems, news items, social media posts, photographs, podcasts and videos. Thanks also to the publishers, agents and persons with disability and their family members who granted me permission to use these excerpts in my book.

Thanks also go to various people closer to home who provided input, wittingly or unwittingly. Most of the excerpts I chose to use were ones that I was already aware of or which I found in the course of my research on appropriate texts to use. A few of them I got to know through others. I therefore thank my husband Ivan for suggesting that I read Kazuo Ishiguro's *Klara and the Sun*; Claire Azzopardi Lane for giving me the Maltese translation of Giacomo Mazzariol's *Mio Fratello Rincorre i Dinosauri*; my sister Marvene Cassar for suggesting that I read Jaap Robben's *Summer Brother*; and Kurt Borg for pointing me to critical phenomenology, suggesting Paul Ricoeur's *Oneself as Another* and forwarding me Eva Kittay's Facebook post about her daughter Sesha on Rare Disease Day.

I also thank my husband Ivan and Kurt Borg for their valued feedback on an early draft of the introductory chapter and on the finished manuscript. Thanks to Denise Chircop, who checked my translations of the French and Italian originals of two of the excerpts; to Michele Moore for her advice, early on, regarding my ideas for the book; to Vickie Gauci for her feedback on my plan for the book and on the first chapters; and again to Vickie and to Amy Camilleri Zahra for being such great colleagues and for making our Department for Disability Studies such a collegial place to work in.

It is only appropriate that I thank my husband Ivan for a third time because my self is so closely bound with his. The debt of gratitude I owe him goes far beyond what could be articulated here.

REFERENCES

AAIDD (2021). *Intellectual disability: Definition, diagnosis, classification, and systems of support* (12th edition). Edited by R. L. Schalock, R. Luckasson and M. J. Tassé. American Association on Intellectual and Developmental Disabilities.

Abela, M. 2012. *The social inclusion of students with moderate to severe disabilities in a boys' comprehensive secondary school: A qualitative study.* Unpublished Masters Dissertation. University of Malta.

Abrams, T. 2020. Disability at the limits of phenomenology. *Puncta*, 3(2), pp. 15–18.

Altermark. 2017. The post-institutional era: Visions of history in research on intellectual disability. *Disability & Society*, 32(9), pp. 1315–1332.

Altermark, N. 2018. *Citizenship Inclusion and intellectual disability: Biopolitics post-institutionalisation.* Routledge.

American Speech-Language-Hearing Association. 2023. Augmentative and alternative communication (AAC). [online]. [Accessed on 22 January 2025]. https://www.asha.org/public/speech/disorders/aac/.

Anchor Films 2015. *Lauren Potter wants you to stop saying 'the r-word'.* [online]. [Accessed on 22 January 2025]. https://anchorfilms.com/lauren-potter-psa/.

Arc of the United States. 2022. *Grief and loss in the lives of people with intellectual and developmental disabilities.* YouTube [online]. [Accessed on 22 January 2025]. https://www.youtube.com/watch?v=Pa7OOAFnj0w.

Arnstein, S. R. 2019. A ladder of citizen participation. *Journal of the American Planning Association*, 85(1), pp. 24–34.

Australian Government Attorney-General's Department. 2017. Marriage equality in Australia. [online]. [Accessed on 22 January 2025]. https://www.ag.gov.au/families-and-marriage/marriage/marriage-equality-australia.

Back to Back Theatre. 2009. *Ganesh versus the Third Reich.* [online]. [Accessed on 22 January 2025]. https://backtobacktheatre.com/project/ganesh/.

Baldacchino, I. 2018. Devising dance performances with adults with learning disabilities. In J. Butterworth (ed.), *Opening doors to the performing arts: Difference and diversity.* Opening Doors Malta, pp. 113–136.

Baldacchino, L. 2018. Opening Doors Music Group: An exciting venture and a true privilege. In J. Butterworth (ed.), *Opening doors to the performing arts: Difference and diversity.* Opening Doors Malta, pp. 77–96.

Barnes, E. 2016. *The minority body: A theory of disability*. Oxford University Press.
Bendukurthi, N. and Raman, U. 2020. What's it all worth? The political economy of disability representation in Indian media. In K. Ellis, G. Goggin, B. Haller and R. Curtis (eds), *The Routledge companion to disability and media*. Routledge, pp. 22–34.
Berlin Hallrup, L., Kumlien, C. and Carlson, E. 2019. Service managers' experiences of how the participation of people with intellectual disabilities can be promoted in Swedish group homes. *Journal of Applied Research in Intellectual Disabilities*, 32(2), pp. 427–434.
Bérubé, M. 1998. *Life as we know it: A father, a family, and an exceptional child*. Vintage.
Bérubé, M. 2016. *Life as Jamie knows it: An exceptional child grows up*. Beacon.
Best Buddies International. 2012. *BBLC: Inclusion revolution – Lauren Potter*. YouTube [online]. [Accessed on 22 January 2025]. https://www.youtube.com/watch?v=5JP1nDfrtUc.
Bingham, A., Correa, V. I. and Huber, J. J. 2012. Mothers' voices: Coping with their children's initial disability diagnosis. *Infant Mental Health Journal*, 33(4), pp. 372–385.
Björnsdóttir, K., Stefánsdóttir, G. V. and Stefánsdóttir, Á. 2015. 'It's my life': Autonomy and people with intellectual disabilities. *Journal of Intellectual Disabilities*, 19(1), pp. 5–21.
Blatt, B. and Kaplan, F. 1974. *Christmas in purgatory: A photographic essay on mental retardation*. Human Policy Press.
Bogdan, R. 2012. *Picturing disability: Beggar, freak, citizen and other photographic rhetoric*. Syracuse University Press.
Bogdan, R. and Taylor, S. T. 1982. *Inside out: The social meaning of mental retardation*. University of Toronto Press.
Bolt, D. 2018. *Cultural disability studies in education: Interdisciplinary navigations of the normative divide*. Routledge.
Borkman, T. 1976. Experiential knowledge: A new concept for the analysis of self-help groups. *Social Service Review*, 50(3), pp. 445–456.
Brady, N. C., Bruce, S., Goldman, A., Erickson, K., Mineo, B., Ogletree, B. T., Paul, D., Romski, M., Sevcik, R., Siegel, E., Schoonover, J., Snell, M., Sylvester, L. and Wilkinson, K. 2016. Communication services and supports for individuals with severe disabilities: Guidance for assessment and intervention. *American Journal on Intellectual and Developmental Disabilities*, 121(2), pp. 121–138.
Brake (n.d.). Supporting bereaved people with learning disabilities. [online]. [Accessed on 22 January 2025]. https://www.brake.org.uk/get-involved/for-professionals/professionals-supporting-victims/tools-and-guidance-for-professionals-supporting-road-victims/supporting-bereaved-people-with-learning-disabilities.
Brand, F., Scior, K. and Loewenberger, A., 2024. Understanding experiences of 'Gig Buddies': A befriending scheme for people with intellectual disabilities. *Journal of Applied Research in Intellectual Disabilities*, 37(3), pp. 1–11.
Bruner, J. S. 1990. *Acts of meaning: Four lectures on mind and culture* (Vol. 3). Harvard University Press.
Bryant, C. D. and Peck, D. L. 2009. Disenfranchised grief. In C. D. Bryant and D. L. Peck (eds), *Encyclopedia of death and the human experience*. SAGE Publications, pp. 379–381.
Buchanan, I. and Walmsley, J. 2006. Self-advocacy in historical perspective. *British Journal of Learning Disabilities*, 34(3), pp. 133–138.
Buhagiar, S. and Azzopardi Lane, C. 2022. Freedom from financial abuse: Persons with intellectual disability discuss protective strategies aimed at empowerment and supported decision-making. *Disability & Society*, 37(3), pp. 361–385.

Bunkers, S.S. 2021. Thoughts on friendship. *Nursing Science Quarterly*, 34(2), pp. 107–112.
Burke, M. M., Rios, K., Aleman-Tovar, J., Lee, C. E., Arnold, C. K. and Owen, A. 2020. Exploring the nature and correlates of caregiving among parents of adults with intellectual and developmental disabilities. *Journal of Applied Research in Intellectual Disabilities*, 33(6), pp. 1259–1267.
Butler, J., 2020. *Senses of the subject*. Fordham University Press.
Callus, A. M. and Cauchi, D. 2020. Ensuring meaningful access to easy-to-read information: A case study. *British Journal of Learning Disabilities*, 48(2), pp. 124–131.
Campbell, J. and Oliver, M. 1996. *Disability politics: Understanding our past, changing our future*. Routledge.
Cardona, G. 2011. Inclusive education: A special right? Commonwealth Educational Partnerships.
Carey, A. C. 2009. *On the margins of citizenship: Intellectual disability and civil rights in twentieth-century America*. Temple University Press.
Carlson, L. 2010. *The faces of intellectual disability: Philosophical reflections*. Indiana University Press.
Carlson, L. 2023. Intellectual disability, dehumanization and the fate of 'the human'. *Journal of Philosophy of Disability*, 3, pp. 47–70.
Centre for Constitutional Studies. 2019. Positive and negative rights. [online]. [Accessed on 22 January 2025]. https://www.constitutionalstudies.ca/2019/07/positive-and-negative-rights/.
Chappell, A. L., Goodley, D. and Lawthom, R. 2001. Making connections: The relevance of the social model of disability for people with learning difficulties. *British Journal of Learning Disabilities*, 29(2), pp. 45–50.
Charlton, J. 2000. *Nothing about us without us*. University of California Press.
Cheng, C., Oakman, J., Bigby, C., Fossey, E., Cavanagh, J., Meacham, H. and Bartram, T. 2018. What constitutes effective support in obtaining and maintaining employment for individuals with intellectual disability? A scoping review. *Journal of Intellectual and Developmental Disability*, 43(3), pp. 317–327.
Choi, H. and Van Riper, M. 2020. Health family adaptation intervention for families of young children with Down syndrome: A feasibility study. *Journal of Pediatric Nursing*, 50, e69–e76.
Coe, M. and Coe, R. 2022. *brother. do. you. love. me.* Little Toller Books.
Committee on the Rights of Persons with Disabilities. 2014. General comment No. 1 on Article 12 – Equal recognition before the law. [online]. [Accessed on 22 January 2025]. https://documents.un.org/doc/undoc/gen/g14/031/20/pdf/g1403120.pdf.
Committee on the Rights of Persons with Disabilities. 2015. Guidelines on article 14 of the Convention on the Rights of Persons with Disabilities – The right to liberty and security of persons with disabilities. [online]. [Accessed on 22 January 2025]. https://www.ohchr.org/Documents/HRBodies/CRPD/GC/GuidelinesArticle14.doc.
Committee on the Rights of Persons with Disabilities. 2016. General comment No. 4 on Article 24 – The right to inclusive education. [online]. [Accessed on 22 January 2025]. https://www.ohchr.org/en/documents/general-comments-and-recommendations/general-comment-no-4-article-24-right-inclusive.
Committee on the Rights of Persons with Disabilities. 2017. General comment No. 5 on Article 19 – The right to live independently and be included in the community. [online]. [Accessed on 22 January 2025]. https://www.ohchr.org/en/documents/general-comments-and-recommendations/general-comment-no5-article-19-right-live.
Committee on the Rights of Persons with Disabilities. 2022. Guidelines on deinstitu tionalization, including in emergencies. [online]. [Accessed on 22 January 2025].

https://www.ohchr.org/en/documents/legal-standards-and-guidelines/crpdc5-guidelines-deinstitutionalization-including.

Constantine, A., Condliffe, R., Clift, P., Tulloh, R., Jansen, K. and Dimopoulos, K. 2021. Cardiac disease in Down Syndrome: Literature review and international expert consensus in collaboration with Down Syndrome International (DSi). *Journal of Congenital Cardiology*, 5, Art. 2, pp. 1–3.

Convention on the Rights of Persons with Disabilities. 2006. [online]. [Accessed on 22 January 2025]. https://www.un.org/disabilities/documents/convention/convoptprot-e.pdf.

Corsano, P., Musetti, A., Guidotti, L. and Capelli, F., 2017. Typically developing adolescents' experience of growing up with a brother with an autism spectrum disorder. *Journal of Intellectual and Developmental Disability*, 42(2), pp. 151–161.

Danielsson, H., Henry, L., Messer, D., Carney, D. P. and Rönnberg, J. 2016. Developmental delays in phonological recoding among children and adolescents with Down syndrome and Williams syndrome. *Research in Developmental Disabilities*, 55, pp. 64–76.

Davies, I., Iriate, E.G., Jarrett, S., Johnson, K., Stainton, T., Tilley, L. and Walmsley, J. 2022. Fifty years of the *British Journal of Learning Disabilities*: The power of the past. *British Journal of Learning Disabilities*, 50(2), pp. 119–121.

Davy, L. 2015. Philosophical inclusive design: Intellectual disability and the limits of individual autonomy in moral and political theory. *Hypatia*, 30(1), pp. 132–148.

Deans, M., Ferguson, M., Gladwin, B., Holland, N., Laherty, S., Mainwaring, S., Price, S., Sulan, K., Tilley, B. and Woods, D. 2013. *Ganesh versus the Third Reich*. In H. Grehan and P. Eckersall (eds), *'We're people who do shows'. Back to Back Theatre: Performance, politics, visibility*. Performance Research Books, pp. 158–194.

Deater-Deckard, K., Pike, A., Petrill, S. A., Cutting, A. L., Hughes, C. and O'Connor, T. G. 2001. Nonshared environmental processes in social-emotional development: An observational study of identical twin differences in the preschool period. *Developmental Science*, 4(2), pp. F1–F6.

Del Giudice, E. et al. 2006. Early intervention for children with Down syndrome in southern Italy: The role of parent-implemented developmental training. *Infants and Young Children*, 19(1), pp. 50–58.

Devi, N. 2013. Supported decision-making and personal autonomy for persons with intellectual disabilities: Article 12 of the UN Convention on the Rights of Persons with Disabilities. *Journal of Law, Medicine and Ethics*, 41(4), pp. 792–806.

DNA Today. 2022, 18 March. #176: Glee's Lauren Potter on Down Syndrome Awareness. [online]. [Accessed on 22 January 2025]. http://dnapodcast.com/episodes/2022/3/18/176-glees-lauren-potter-on-down-syndrome-awareness.

Dodd, P., Dowling, S. and Hollins, S., 2005. A review of the emotional, psychiatric and behavioural responses to bereavement in people with intellectual disabilities. *Journal of Intellectual Disability Research*, 49(7), pp. 537–543.

Doka. K. J. 2018, 30 November. Is there a right to grieve? Enfranchising the disenfranchised. *Psychology Today*. [Accessed on 22 January 2025]. https://www.psychologytoday.com/gb/blog/good-mourning/201811/is-there-right-grieve.

Doran, N. 2014. Me. In *Pen & Palette: A selection of poetry of paintings by students of the National Institute for Intellectual Disability, Trinity College, Dublin*. Trinity College, Dublin, p. 18.

Dovigo, F. (ed.) 2017. *Special educational needs and inclusive practices: An international perspective*. Springer.

Down Syndrome Australia. 2022. Getting ready to vote. [online]. [Accessed on 22 January 2025]. https://www.downsyndrome.org.au/national/wp-content/uploads/sites/12/2022/03/DSA-Voting_Easy-Read_PDF_2022.pdf.

Dunn, M. C., Clare, I. C. and Holland, A. J. 2010. Living 'a life like ours': Support workers' accounts of substitute decision-making in residential care homes for adults with intellectual disabilities. *Journal of Intellectual Disability Research*, 54(2), pp. 144–160.

EASNIE 2021. Country policy review and analysis: Key messages for working *with* and *for* countries. [online]. [Accessed on 22 January 2025]. https://www.european-agency.org/sites/default/files/Country_Policy_Review_and_Analysis.pdf.

Ellenkamp, J. J., Brouwers, E. P., Embregts, P. J., Joosen, M. C. and van Weeghel, J. 2016. Work environment-related factors in obtaining and maintaining work in a competitive employment setting for employees with intellectual disabilities: A systematic review. *Journal of Occupational Rehabilitation*, 26(1), pp. 56–69.

Ellis, L. 2017. Reclaiming kith: Weaving belongingness into community. In K. Soldatic and K. Johnson (eds), *Disability and rurality: Identity, gender and belonging*. Routledge, pp. 215–232.

European Parliament. 2024. European elections 2024. [online]. [Accessed on 22 January 2025]. https://together.europarl.europa.eu/download-centre.

Evenbreak. 2022. How job carving can help disabled employees and the organisation. [online]. [Accessed on 22 January 2025]. https://blog.evenbreak.co.uk/2019/03/06/how-job-carving-can-help-disabled-employees-and-the-organisation/.

Forster, S. and Iacono, T. 2008. Disability support workers' experience of interaction with a person with profound intellectual disability. *Journal of Intellectual and Developmental Disability*, 33(2), pp. 137–147.

Fraser, B. 2018. *Cognitive disability aesthetics: Visual culture, disability representations, and the (in)visibility of cognitive difference*. University of Toronto Press.

Fraser, B., 2021. Down syndrome ensembles, autonomy and disability rights in Maite Alberdi's *The Grown-Ups* (2016). *Chasqui*, 50(2), pp. 233–252.

Fullana, J., Pallisera, M. and Díaz-Garolera, G. 2019. How do people with learning disabilities talk about professionals and organizations? Discourse on support practices for independent living, *Disability & Society*, 34(9–10), pp. 1462–1480.

Fundamental Rights Agency. 2024. *Political participation of people with disabilities: New developments*. [online]. [Accessed on 22 January 2025]. https://fra.europa.eu/en/publication/2024/political-participation.

García Iriarte, E., O'Brien, P., McConkey, R., Wolfe, M. and O'Doherty, S. 2014. Identifying the key concerns of Irish persons with intellectual disability. *Journal of Applied Research in Intellectual Disabilities*, 27(6), pp. 564–575.

Garland-Thomson, R. 1997. *Extraordinary bodies: Figuring physical disability in American culture and literature*. Columbia University Press.

Garrels, V. and Sigstad, H. M. H. 2019. Motivation for employment in Norwegian adults with mild intellectual disability: The role of competence, autonomy, and relatedness. *Scandinavian Journal of Disability Research*, 21(1), pp. 250–261.

Ghirlando, L. 2018. Presence and the role of the facilitator. In J. Butterworth (ed.), *Opening doors to the performing arts: Difference and diversity*. Opening Doors Malta, pp. 97–112.

Gladwin, B. and Gough, R. 2013. Making room for elephants. In H. Grehan and P. Eckersall (eds), *'We're people who do shows'. Back to Back Theatre: Performance, politics, visibility*. Performance Research Books, pp. 231–257.

Goffman, E. 1961. *Asylums: Essays on the condition of the social situation of mental patients and other inmates*. Anchor Books.

Goode, D. A. 1984. Socially produced identities, intimacy and the problem of competence among the retarded. In L. Barton and S. Tomlinson (eds), *Special education and social interests*. Routledge, pp. 228–248.

Gordy, S. 2020. Champagne, snakes and stealing chips. In S. Salman (ed.), *Made possible: Stories of success by people with learning disabilities – in their own words*. Unbound Publishing, pp. 50–62.

Grant, G., Ramcharan, P. and Flynn, M. (eds), 2010. *Learning disability: A life cycle approach*. McGraw-Hill.

Griffiths, C. and Smith, M. 2016. Attuning: A communication process between people with severe and profound intellectual disability and their interaction partners. *Journal of Applied Research in Intellectual Disabilities*, 29(2), pp. 124–138.

Guddingsmo, H. 2022. Growing a method for empowerment with applied theatre. *Disability & Society*, 39(3), pp. 642–662.

Hamer, J. 2019, 9 September. Grief hierarchy: Who has a right to grieve? Marie Curie. [online]. [Accessed on 22 January 2025]. https://www.mariecurie.org.uk/blog/grief-hierarchy-who-has-the-right-to-grieve.

Harry, M. L., MacDonald, L., McLuckie, A., Battista, C., Mahoney, E. K. and Mahoney, K. J. 2017. Long-term experiences in cash and counseling for young adults with intellectual disabilities: Familial programme representative descriptions. *Journal of Applied Research in Intellectual Disabilities*, 30(4), pp. 573–583.

Harvey, K. 2023. *Trauma and healing in the lives of people with intellectual disability*. American Association on Intellectual and Developmental Disabilities.

Helenius, T. 2021. Paul Ricœur: A phenomenological hermeneutics of meaningful action. In C. Erhard and T. Keiling (eds), *The Routledge handbook of phenomenology of agency*. Routledge, pp. 189–207.

Helm, B. 2021. Friendship. *The Stanford encyclopedia of philosophy* (Fall 2023 Edition), E. N. Zalta and U. Nodelman (eds). [online]. [Accessed on 22 January 2025]. https://plato.stanford.edu/archives/fall2023/entries/friendship.

Hepburn, M. A. 2014. *Lives worthy of life and remembrance: Memorialization of the National Socialist Aktion T4 euthanasia programme*. PhD thesis, University of Toronto. [online]. [Accessed on 22 January 2025]. https://tspace.library.utoronto.ca/bitstream/1807/72506/1/Hepburn_Meaghan_A_201406_PhD_thesis.pdf.

Hodge, N., and Runswick-Cole, K., 2013. 'They never pass me the ball': Exposing ableism through the leisure experiences of disabled children, young people and their families. *Children's Geographies*, 11(3), pp. 311–325.

Hollomotz, A. 2014. Are we 'valuing people's' choices 'now'? Restrictions to mundane choices made by adults with learning difficulties. *British Journal of Social Work*, 44(2), pp. 234–251.

Hostyn, I., Petry, K., Lambrechts, G. and Maes, B. 2011. Evaluating the quality of the interaction between persons with profound intellectual and multiple disabilities and direct support staff: A preliminary application of three observation scales from parent–infant research. *Journal of Applied Research in Intellectual Disabilities*, 24(5), pp. 407–420.

Hsiao, C. Y. and Van Riper, M. 2011. Individual and family adaptation in Taiwanese families living with Down syndrome. *Journal of Family Nursing*, 17(2), pp. 182–201.

Inclusion Europe. 2009. *Information for all: European standards for making information easy to read and understand*. [online]. [Accessed on 22 January 2025]. https://www.inclusion-europe.eu/wp-content/uploads/2017/06/EN_Information_for_all.pdf.

Inclusion Europe. 2020a. My talents. For diversity. [online]. [Accessed on 22 January 2025]. https://www.inclusion-europe.eu/videos-employment-people-with-disabilities/.

Inclusion Europe. 2020b. *Customised employment*. YouTube [online]. [Accessed on 22 January 2025]. https://www.youtube.com/watch?v=4hVg4K65KCA.

Inclusion International. 2018. Inclusion: Myths and misconceptions. [online]. [Accessed on 20 January 2025]. https://s38312.pcdn.co/wp-content/uploads/Catalyst-Myths-and-Misconceptions.pdf.

Inclusion Melbourne. 2018. *I can vote*. Shae [*sic*] MacDonough. YouTube [online]. [Accessed on 20 January 2025]. https://www.youtube.com/watch?app=desktop&v=92_5JYiNjIg.

International IDEA (n.d.). Compulsory voting. [online]. [Accessed on 22 January 2025]. https://www.idea.int/data-tools/data/voter-turnout-database/compulsory-voting.

Ishiguro, K. 2021. *Klara and the sun*. Faber & Faber.
It Starts With a Voice. 2013. *Be the One starring GLEE's Lauren Potter*. YouTube. [online]. [Accessed on 20 January 2025]. https://www.youtube.com/watch?v=GPlyMkWulx8.
Jack N John. 2015. *The simple interview*. YouTube [online]. [Accessed on 20 January 2025]. https://www.youtube.com/watch?v=0v8twxPsszY.
Jackson, I., Dagnan, D., Golding, L. and Rayner-Smith, K. 2024. How do people with intellectual disabilities understand friendship? A systematic meta-synthesis. *Journal of Applied Research in Intellectual Disabilities*, 37(4), e13244. https://doi.org/10.1111/jar.13244.
Jacobson, K., 2020. Spatiality and agency: A phenomenology of containment. *Puncta*, 3(2), pp. 54–75.
Jansen, S. L., van der Putten, A. A. and Vlaskamp, C. 2017. Parents' experiences of collaborating with professionals in the support of their child with profound intellectual and multiple disabilities: A multiple case study. *Journal of Intellectual Disabilities*, 21(1), pp. 53–67.
Jarrett, S. 2020. *Those they called idiots: The idea of the disabled mind from 1700 to the present day*. Reaktion.
Josol, C. K., Fisher, M. H. and Athamanah, L. S. 2023. Perspectives of adults without disabilities on their friendships with individuals with intellectual and developmental disabilities. *Journal of Intellectual Disabilities*, 27(3), pp. 613–632.
Kamstra, A., Van der Putten, A. A. J., Post, W. J. and Vlaskamp, C. 2015. Informal social networks of people with profound intellectual and multiple disabilities: Relationship with age, communicative abilities and current living arrangements. *Journal of Applied Research in Intellectual Disabilities*, 28(2), pp. 159–164.
Keeley, J., Mancini, V. O., Castell, E. and Breen, J. L. 2023. The neglect of a child with intellectual disability as reported in Australian news media: A Foucauldian discourse analysis. *Disability & Society*, 39(7), pp. 1682–1704.
Keller, S. 2023. Beyond ideals of friendship. *Journal of Applied Philosophy*, 41(3), pp. 549–565.
King, J. 2021, 29 October. Schoolchildren made to do PE barefoot so they didn't ruin posh new floor. *Metro*. [online]. [Accessed on 22 January 2025]. https://metro.co.uk/2021/10/29/schoolchildren-made-to-do-pe-barefoot-so-they-didnt-ruin-new-floor-15511450/.
Kingsley, E. P. 1987. Welcome to Holland. [Accessed on 22 January 2025]. https://www.emilyperlkingsley.com/welcome-to-holland.
Kittay, E. F. 2017. The moral significance of being human. *Proceedings and Addresses of the American Philosophical Association*, 91, pp. 22–42.
Kittay, E. F. 2019a. *Love's labor: Essays on women, equality and dependency* (2nd edition). Routledge.
Kittay, E. F. 2019b. *Learning from my daughter: The value and care of disabled minds*. Oxford University Press.
Kittay, E. F. 2024, 29 February. Untitled Facebook post. [online]. [Accessed on 22 January 2025]. https://www.facebook.com/1362986703/posts/pfbid0GTc8pt-tW4TvDruKPJ3bzsNiEoDT13Pack2sMF5pHawvN5fHsQqKBkFF6tqHatCTSl/.
Kittay, E. F. and Kittay, L. B. 2000. On the expressivity and ethics of selective abortion for disability: Conversations with my son. In A. Asch and E. Parens (eds), *The ethics of prenatal testing and selective abortion: A report from the Hastings Center*. [online]. [Accessed on 22 January 2025]. https://evafederkittay.com/wp-content/uploads/2014/11/ExpressivityCompleteOCR.pdf.
Kruithof, K., Ijzerman, L., Nieuwenhuijse, A., Huisman, S., Schippers, A., Willems, D. and Olsman, E. 2021. Siblings' and parents' perspectives on the future care for their family member with profound intellectual and multiple disabilities: A qualitative study. *Journal of Intellectual and Developmental Disability*, 46(4), pp. 351–361.

Kruithof, K., Willems, D., van Etten-Jamaludin, F. and Olsman, E. 2020. Parents' knowledge of their child with profound intellectual and multiple disabilities: An interpretative synthesis. *Journal of Applied Research in Intellectual Disabilities*, 33(6), pp. 1141–1150.

Lacherelle, M. 2023. *Être parent d'un adulte en situation d'handicap: Grandir ensemble* [*Being a parent of an adult with disability: Growing up together*]. Érès.

Lansade, G. 2019. De la difficulté à être reconnus 'capables' et 'compétents': Des adolescents et jeunes adultes désignés handicapés mentaux en quéte d'autonomie [The difficulty of being recognized as 'capable' and 'competent': Adolescents and young adults designated as mentally disabled in search of autonomy]. *Alter: European Journal of Disability Research*, 13(1), pp. 29–42.

Loreman, T. 2014. Measuring inclusive education outcomes in Alberta, Canada. *International Journal of Inclusive Education*, 18(5), pp. 459–483.

Luijkx, J., Van Der Putten, A. A. and Vlaskamp, C. 2016. 'I love my sister, but sometimes I don't': A qualitative study into the experiences of siblings of a child with profound intellectual and multiple disabilities. *Journal of Intellectual and Developmental Disability*, 41(4), pp. 279–288.

Mander, C. 2015. First-hand experience of accessible information. *Tizard Learning Disability Review*, 20(2), pp. 80–87.

Mansell, J. and Ericsson, K. 1996. *Deinstitutionalisation and community living: Intellectual disability services in Scandinavia, Britain and the USA*. Chapman & Hall.

Mansfield, N. 2020. *Subjectivity: Theories of the self from Freud to Haraway*. Routledge.

Martin, A. M., Andrews, T., Goldbart, J. and Landers, M. 2022. Reconciling communication repertoires: Navigating interactions involving persons with severe/profound intellectual disability, a classic grounded theory study. *Journal of Intellectual Disability Research*, 66(4), pp. 332–352.

Mazzariol, G. 2020. *Mio fratello rincorre i dinosauri* [*My brother chases dinosaurs*]. Giulio Einaudi.

McConkey, R. and Lorenzo, T. 2022. Leisure and friendship. In H. Atherton and D. Crickmore (eds), *Intellectual disabilities: Toward inclusion* (7th edition). Elsevier, pp. 381–396.

McKenzie, K., Ouellette Kuntz, H., Blinkhorn, A. and Demoré, A. 2017. Out of school and into distress: Families of young adults with intellectual and developmental disabilities in transition. *Journal of Applied Research in Intellectual Disabilities*, 30(4), pp. 774–781.

McMahan, J. 2003. *The ethics of killing: Problems as the margins of life*. Oxford University Press.

McRitchie, R., McKenzie, K., Quayle, E., Harlin, M. and Neumann, K. 2014. How adults with an intellectual disability experience bereavement and grief: A qualitative exploration. *Death Studies*, 38(3), pp. 179–185.

McVilly, K., Anderson, J., Koritsas, S., Johnson, H., Wiese, M. and Stancliffe, R. 2018. Accessible written information resources for adults with intellectual disability: Compiling the evidence to inform good practice. *Journal of Applied Research in Intellectual Disabilities*, 31(4), pp. 594–594.

Media Access Awards (2012). 2012 Media Access Awards. [online]. [Accessed on 22 January 2025]. https://mediaaccessawards.com/awards/2012-media-access-awards/.

Meltzer, A., Robinson, S. and Fisher, K. R. 2020. Barriers to finding and maintaining open employment for people with intellectual disability in Australia. *Social Policy and Administration*, 54(1), pp. 88–101.

Merrells, J., Buchanan, A. and Waters, R. 2019. 'We feel left out': Experiences of social inclusion from the perspective of young adults with intellectual disability. *Journal of Intellectual and Developmental Disability*, 44(1), pp. 13–22.

Miller, G. 2013. *Six percent – Down's syndrome: My photographs their stories*. Photohonesty.
Minjee, K. 2019. The right to grieve. *JAMA*, 321(16), pp. 1569–1570.
Morgan, H. 2022. *The joy of knowing Pete: Much was said, yet no words were spoken*. YouCaxton Publications.
Morris, J. 1993. *Independent lives? Community care and disabled people*. Macmillan. [online]. [Accessed on 22 January 2025]. https://disability-studies.leeds.ac.uk/wp-content/uploads/sites/40/library/Independent%20lives.pdf.
Moyà-Köhler, J. 2024. Exploring independent living initiatives for people with intellectual disabilities: Insights from the Spanish case. *Disability & Society*, pp. 1–22. https://doi.org/10.1080/09687599.2024.2368559.
Moyson, T. and Roeyers, H. 2012. 'The overall quality of my life as a sibling is all right, but of course, it could always be better'. Quality of life of siblings of children with intellectual disability: The siblings' perspectives. *Journal of Intellectual Disability Research*, 56(1), pp. 87–101.
Nelson, J. (dir.) 2001. *I Am Sam*. [DVD]. The Bedford Falls Company.
Niedbalski, J., 2022. The institutional conditions of the life of people with intellectual disabilities (ID) in a residential care facility. *Przegląd Socjologii Jakościowej*, 18(2), pp. 72–88.
Nietupski, J. A. and Hamre-Nietupski, S. 2000. A systematic process for carving supported employment positions for people with severe disabilities. *Journal of Developmental and Physical Disabilities*, 12, pp. 103–119.
Nijs, S. and Maes, B. 2021. Assistive technology for persons with profound intellectual disability: A European survey on attitudes and beliefs. *Disability and Rehabilitation: Assistive Technology*, 16(5), pp. 497–504.
Nouwen, H. J. 2022. *Adam: God's beloved*. Orbis.
Nussbaum, M. C. 2006. *Frontiers of justice*. Harvard University Press.
Nussbaum, M. C. 2009. The capabilities of people with cognitive disabilities. In E. F. Kittay and L. Carlson (eds), *Cognitive disability and its challenge to moral philosophy*. Wiley-Blackwell, pp. 75–96.
O'Brien, J. and Duffy, S. 2022. In H. Atherton and D. Crickmore (eds), *Intellectual disabilities: Toward inclusion* (7th edition). Elsevier, pp. 37–52.
Ogletree, B. T., McMurry, S., Schmidt, M. and Evans, K. 2018. The changing world of augmentative and alternative communication (AAC): Examining three realities faced by today's AAC provider. *Perspectives of the ASHA Special Interest Groups*, 3(12), pp. 113–122.
Opening Doors Association. (n.d.). Welcome to Opening Doors. [online]. [Accessed on 22 January 2025]. https://openingdoors.org.mt.
Oliver, M. 1990. *The politics of disablement*. Macmillan.
Osgood, T. 2019. *Supporting positive behaviour in intellectual disabilities and autism: Practical strategies for addressing challenging behaviour*. Jessica Kingsley.
PAMIS. 2017. *Profound inclusion*. YouTube. [online]. [Accessed on 22 January 2025]. https://www.youtube.com/watch?v=Ekhpi-g8gDQ.
Parenting Special Needs. 2016, 10 March. Lauren Potter stars in a film about intimacy and Down syndrome. [online]. [Accessed on 22 January 2025]. https://www.parentingspecialneeds.org/article/lauren-potter-stars-guest-room-film-intimacy-syndrome/print/.
Park, E. Y. 2022. Factors affecting labour market transitions, sustained employment and sustained unemployment in individuals with intellectual disabilities. *Journal of Applied Research in Intellectual Disabilities*, 35(1), pp. 271–279.
Parks, M., Priest, H., Dodd, P., Forrester-Jones, R., Bowman, T., Larkin, P. J., Wiese, M., Brown, E., Machin, L., Blackman, N. and Gaventa, W. 2014. *Supporting people with intellectual disabilities experiencing loss and bereavement: Theory and compassionate practice*. Jessica Kingsley.

Pavlopoulou, G., Burns, C., Cleghorn, R., Skyrla, T. and Avnon, J. 2022. 'I often have to explain to school staff what she needs': School experiences of non-autistic siblings growing up with an autistic brother or sister. *Research in Developmental Disabilities*, 129, Art. 104323.

Pérez-Curiel P., Vicente E., Morán M. L. and Gómez, L. E. 2023. The right to sexuality, reproductive health, and found a family for people with intellectual disability: A systematic review. International Journal of Environmental Research and Public Health, 20(2), 1587.

Phelan, M. 2019. Rethinking friendship. *Inquiry*, 66(5), pp. 757–772.

Phillips, S. 2018. *A world without Down syndrome*. YouTube [online]. [Accessed on 22 January 2025]. https://www.youtube.com/watch?v=45am4xYR_-4.

Piepmeier, A. 2021. *Unexpected: Parenting, prenatal testing, and Down syndrome*. NYU Press.

Pleven, L. and Callus, A. M. 2017. The outcomes of mainstream post-secondary education for young people with intellectual disability: Investing in human capital or whiling away the time? *Malta Review of Educational Research*, 11(2), pp. 223–241.

Povee, K., Roberts, L., Bourke, J. and Leonard, H. 2012. Family functioning in families with a child with Down syndrome: A mixed methods approach. *Journal of Intellectual Disability Research*, 56(10), pp. 961–973.

Power, A. and Bartlett, R. 2018. 'I shouldn't be living there because I am a sponger': Negotiating everyday geographies by people with learning disabilities. *Disability & Society*, 33(4), pp. 562–578.

Premio Sciacca. 2016. YouTube [online]. [Accessed on 22 January 2025]. https://www.youtube.com/watch?v=UdTgw-EfAKA.

Prior, Y. 2013. 'Scott's aired a couple of things': Back to Back Theatre rehearse *Ganesh Versus the Third Reich*. In H. Grehan and P. Eckersall (eds), *'We're people who do shows'. Back to Back Theatre: Performance, politics, visibility*. Performance Research Books, pp. 209–217.

Quora. 2021. If a teacher says take your socks off in school gym, is that okay because I don't want to show my feet to the girls because there was a time where they want to touch my feet and I hated it? [online]. [Accessed on 22 January 2025] https://www.quora.com/If-a-teacher-says-take-your-socks-off-in-school-gym-is-that-okay-because-I-don-t-want-to-show-my-feet-to-the-girls-because-there-was-a-time-where-they-want-to-touch-my-feet-and-I-hated-it.

Rapley, M. 2004. *The social construction of intellectual disability*. Cambridge University Press.

Rare Disease Day. 2024. What is rare disease day? [online]. [Accessed on 22 January 2025]. https://www.rarediseaseday.org/what-is-rare-disease-day/.

Read, S. and Elliott, D. 2003. Death and learning disability: A vulnerability perspective. *Journal of Adult Protection*, 5(1), pp. 5–14.

Read, S. and Wiese, M. 2022. End of life: Holistic approaches to loss, dying and death. In H. Atherton and D. Crickmore (eds), *Intellectual disabilities: Toward inclusion* (7th edition) Elsevier, pp. 483–497.

Reid, B. (dir.) 2019. *Innocence* [Film] SweetDoh! Productions. YouTube. [online]. [Accessed on 22 January 2025]. https://www.youtube.com/watch?v=Rih_GMIjaWI.

Reinders, H. S. 2008. *Receiving the gift of friendship: Profound disability, theological anthropology, and ethics*. Eerdmans.

Ricoeur, P. 1992. *Oneself as another*. University of Chicago Press.

Rieser, R. 2012. Implementing inclusive education: A Commonwealth guide to implementing Article 24 of the UN Convention on the Rights of Persons with Disabilities (2nd edition). Commonwealth Secretariat.

Robben, J. 2021. *Summer brother*. Translated by David Doherty. World Editions.

Rodríguez Díaz, B. 2019. Mission impossible? Preventing discrimination on grounds of disability of foetuses with Down syndrome in Spain after the emergence of non-invasive prenatal testing. *International Journal of Discrimination and the Law*, 19(3–4), pp. 178–199.

Roll, A. E. and Bowers, B. J. 2019. Building and connecting: Family strategies for developing social support networks for adults with Down syndrome. *Journal of Family Nursing*, 25(1), pp. 128–151.

Revillard, A. 2023. *Fragile rights: Disability, public policy, and social change*. Policy Press.

Ryan, F. 2020, 26 March. With rights come responsibilities. The Lincoln Institute. [online]. [Accessed on 22 January 2025]. https://www.lincolninstitute.org/with-rights-come-responsibilities/.

Ryan, K., Guerin, S., Dodd, P. and McEvoy, J. 2011. Exploring the experiences of people with intellectual disabilities when service users die. *British Journal of Learning Disabilities*, 39(4), pp. 259–265.

SAMSHA 2012. *Supported employment – introductory video*. YouTube [online]. [Accessed on 22 January 2025]. https://www.youtube.com/watch?v=DoLO_p04uKY.

Scott, J. (n.d.). Judith & Joyce Scott [online]. [Accessed on 22 January 2025]. https://www.judithandjoyce.com.

Scott, R., Collins, B., Knight, V. and Kleinert, H. 2013. Teaching adults with moderate intellectual disability ATM use via the iPod. *Education and Training in Autism and Developmental Disabilities*, 48(2), pp. 190–199.

Schalock, R. L., Luckasson, R. and Tassé, M. J. (eds) 2021. *Intellectual disability: Definition, diagnosis, classification, and systems of support* (12th edition). American Association on Intellectual and Developmental Disabilities.

Shott, S. R. 2006. Down syndrome: Common otolaryngologic manifestations. *American Journal of Medical Genetics Part C: Seminars in Medical Genetics*, 142(3), pp. 131–140.

Siedlecka-Dorosz, W. 2020. '. . . and we all': The phenomenon of Teatr 21. In K. Ojrzyńska and Maciej Wieczorek (eds), *Disability and dissensus: Strategies of disability representation and inclusion in contemporary culture*. Brill, pp. 200–214.

Simon, R. 2002. *Riding the bus with my sister*. Grand Central Publishing.

Singer, P. 2010. Speciesism and moral status. In E. F. Kittay and L. Carlson (eds), *Cognitive disability and its challenge to moral philosophy*. Wiley-Blackwell, pp. 331–344.

Slee, R. 2012. Revisiting the politics of special educational needs and disability studies in education with Len Barton. In M. Arnot (ed.), *The sociology of disability and inclusive education: A tribute to Len Barton*. Routledge, pp. 34–46.

Snow, K. 2010. Interdependence. [online]. [Accessed on 22 January 2025]. https://nebula.wsimg.com/fb242329f59d3b2a3e768a3d12142a8c?AccessKeyId=9D6F6082FE5EE52C3DC6&disposition=0&alloworigin=1.

Snyder, S. L. and Mitchell, D. T. 2010. *Cultural locations of disability*. University of Chicago Press.

Special Olympics (2015). Lauren Potter. Actor & Advocate. [online]. [Accessed on 22 January 2025]. https://www.specialolympics.org/about/ambassadors/lauren-potter.

Startin, C. M., Rodger, E., Fodor-Wynne, L., Hamburg, S. and Strydom, A. 2016. Developing an informant questionnaire for cognitive abilities in Down syndrome: The Cognitive Scale for Down Syndrome (CS-DS). *PLoS One*, 11(5), e0154596.

Stolen Lives. 2024. Stolen Lives. [online]. [Accessed on 22 January 2025]. https://stolenlives.blog.

Strauss, B. 2015. *The quality of life*. YouTube. [online]. [Accessed on 22 January 2025]. https://www.youtube.com/watch?v=M0EUCyjBmQ8.

Sutcliffe, J. and Simons, K. 1993. *Self-advocacy and adults with learning difficulties*. National Institute of Adult Continuing Education.

Svanelöv, E. and Talman, L. 2022. It is supposed to be a home: Barriers to everyday life decisions in group homes. In H. Egard, K., Hansson, K. and D. Wästerfors (eds), *Accessibility denied: Understanding inaccessibility and everyday resistance to inclusion for persons with disabilities*. Routledge, pp. 159–170.

Tate, J. (dir.) 2015. *The Guest Room* [Film] Cicatrice Pictures. YouTube. [online]. [Accessed on 22 January 2025]. https://www.youtube.com/watch?v=7im7YOY-Tac.

Thomas, C. 2004. Developing the social relational in the social model of disability: A theoretical agenda. In C. Barnes and G. Mercer (eds), *Implementing the social model of disability: Theory and research*. The Disability Press, pp. 32–47.

Thorp, N., Stedmon, J. and Lloyd, H. 2018. 'I carry her in my heart': An exploration of the experience of bereavement for people with learning disability. *British Journal of Learning Disabilities*, 46(1), pp. 45–53.

Titchovsky, T. 2020. Disability imaginaries in the news. In K. Ellis, G. Goggin, B. Haller and R. Curtis (eds), *The Routledge companion to disability and media*. Routledge, pp. 11–22.

Tsokova, D. and Tarr, J. 2012. *Diverse perspectives on inclusive school communities*. Routledge.

UN Special Rapporteur on Disability. 2021. Report of the Special Rapporteur on the rights of persons with disabilities. [online] [Accessed on 18 September 2024]. Available from https://documents.un.org/doc/undoc/gen/g21/012/14/pdf/g2101214.pdf?OpenElement.

UNESCO. 1994. Salamanca Statement and Framework for Action on Special Needs Education. [online]. [Accessed on 22 January 2025]. https://unesdoc.unesco.org/ark:/48223/pf0000098427.

Universal Declaration of Human Rights. 1948 [online]. [Accessed on 22 January 2025]. https://www.un.org/en/about-us/universal-declaration-of-human-rights.

Valentine, D., 2020. Shifting the weight of inaccessibility: Access intimacy as a critical phenomenological ethos. *Puncta*, 3(2), pp. 76–94.

Van Manen, M. 2016a. *Researching lived experience: Human science for an action sensitive pedagogy*. Routledge.

Van Manen, M. 2016b. *Phenomenology of practice: Meaning-giving methods in phenomenological research and writing*. Routledge.

Van Mieghem, A., Verschueren, K., Petry, K. and Struyf, E. 2020. An analysis of research on inclusive education: A systematic search and meta review. *International Journal of Inclusive Education*, 24(6), pp. 675–689.

Van Rens, M., Haelermans, C., Groot, W. and van den Brink, H. M. 2019. Girls' and boys' perceptions of the transition from primary to secondary school. *Child Indicators Research*, 12, pp. 1481–1506.

Vehmas, S. and Riddle, C. A. 2020. What can philosophy tell us about disability? In N. Watson and S. Vehmas (eds), *Routledge handbook of disability studies* (2nd edition). Routledge.

Veraksa, N. and Samuelsson, I. P. (eds) 2022. *Piaget and Vygotsky in XXI century: Discourse in early childhood education*. Springer.

Vlachou, A., Roka, O. and Stavroussi, P. 2021. Experiences of workers with disabilities receiving supported employment services in Greece. *Journal of Intellectual Disabilities*, 25(2), pp. 151–167.

Vuk, M. 2023. *Theological perspectives on reimagining friendship and disability*. Springer.

Weiss, G., Salamon, G. and Murphy, A. V. 2020. *50 Concepts for a critical phenomenology*. Northwestern University Press.

Witsø, A. E. and Hauger, B. 2020. 'It's our everyday life': The perspectives of persons with intellectual disabilities in Norway. *Journal of Intellectual Disabilities*, 24(2), pp. 143–157.

Wright, E. and Edmonds, C. 2022, 13 May. An 'archaic' law has been removing Australians with disability from the electoral roll 'in droves', advocates say. ABC News. [online]. [Accessed on 22 January 2025]. https://www.abc.net.au/news/2022-05-14/disability-voting-laws/101059872.

Young, H., Hogg, J. and Garrard, B. 2017. Making sense of bereavement in people with profound intellectual and multiple disabilities: Carer perspectives. *Journal of Applied Research in Intellectual Disabilities*, 30(6), pp. 1035–1044.

Zambri, I. M., Amin, A. S., Kamil, N. K. M., Akhir, N. M., Sutan, R., Khairuddin, K. F. and Wan, W. A. 2023. Factor affecting independent living of persons with intellectual disabilities: A systematic review. *International Journal of Academic Research in Progressive Education and Development*, 12(1), pp. 623–644.

Zames Fleischer, D. and Zames, F. 2011. *The disability rights movement: From charity to confrontation*. Temple University Press.

INDEX